# The Necessary Going On

Also by Gary Fincke

**Poetry**
*For Now, We Have Been Spared*
*The Mussolini Diaries*
*The Infinity Room*
*After the Three-Moon Era*
*Bringing Back the Bones: New and Selected Poems*
*The History of Permanence*
*Reviving the Dead*
*The Fire Landscape*
*Standing around the Heart*
*Writing Letters for the Blind*
*Blood Ties*
*The Almanac for Desire*
*The Technology of Paradise*
*Inventing Angels*
*The Double Negatives of the Living*
*Plant Voices*
*The Days of Uncertain Health*

**Fiction**
*The History of the Baker's Dozen* (flash)
*After the Locks are Changed* (stories)
*The Corridors of Longing* (flash)
*Nothing Falls from Nowhere* (stories)
*The Sorrows* (stories)
*The Out-of-Sorts: New and Selected Stories*
*The Killer's Dog* (stories)
*A Room of Rain* (stories)
*How Blasphemy Sounds to God* (novel)
*The Proper Words for Sin* (stories)
*Sorry I Worried You* (stories)
*The Stone Child* (stories)
*Emergency Calls* (stories)
*For Keepsies* (stories)

**Nonfiction**
*The Mayan Syndrome* (essays)
*The Darkness Call* (essays)
*Vanishings* (essays)
*The Canals of Mars* (memoir)
*Amp'd: A Father's Backstage Pass* (memoir)

# The Necessary Going On

Selected Poems 1980–2025

# Gary Fincke

Press 53
Winston-Salem

Press 53, LLC
PO Box 30314
Winston-Salem, NC 27130

First Edition

Copyright © 2025 by Gary Fincke

All rights reserved, including the right of reproduction in whole or in part in any form except in the case of brief quotations embodied in critical articles or reviews. For permission, contact publisher at editor@press53.com or at the address above.

Cover photo acquired through Pexels

Cover design by Kevin Morgan Watson

Library of Congress Control Number
(Pending)

ISBN 978-1-950413-97-3

*For all the poets whose work has taught me
what poetry can be*

# Acknowledgments

The author thanks the editors of the publications where these poems first appeared, occasionally in different form:

### A Week of Uncertain Health

"The Girl Who Breathes Through a Hole in Her Throat," *Poetry*
"Quagmire," *Yarrow*
"Street Cleaning," *Memphis State Review*

### Plant Voices

"What the Builder Left," *The Gettysburg Review*
"Groaning Boards," *The Georgia Review*
"Sleeping with the Leper," *Beloit Poetry Journal*
"Bourbon, Red Meat, Salt Grease," *Poetry*
"Ants," *Prairie Schooner*

### The Double Negatives of the Living

"Naming the Sky," *Poetry Northwest*
"The Flower Remedies," *Poetry Northwest*
"The Stuttering Cures," *Poetry*
"The Pet Cemetery," *Zone 3*
"Reaching the Deaf," *Poetry*
"Six Kinds of Music, the Wallpaper of Breasts," *Beloit Poetry Journal*
"The Double Negatives of the Living," *Poetry*

### Inventing Angels

"A Murder of Crows," *Poetry*
"The Book of Numbers," *Poetry Northwest*
"The Wonder Children," *Poetry Northwest*
"The Butterfly Effect," *Green Mountains Review*
"The Skill of the Sunlight's Good," *The Gettysburg Review*
"Every Reachable Feather," *Poetry Northwest*
"Inventing Angels," *The Gettysburg Review*

## The Technology of Paradise

"Hanging the Pigs," *The Gettysburg Review*
"The Cabinet of Wonders," *Mid-American Review*
"The Doctrine of Signatures," *Poetry Northwest*

## The Almanac for Desire

"The Dark Angels," *The Gettysburg Review*
"The Holy Numbers," *DoubleTake*
"The Natural Method for Dog Training," *Verse*
"Schmaltz," *The Missouri Review*
"The Terrors," *Poetry Northwest*
"The Spiritualists," *Press*
"Light Enough to Be Lifted," *Mid-American Review*

## Blood Ties

"The Tentative Steps of the Obese," *Poetry Northwest*
"The Extrapolation Dreams," *The Gettysburg Review*
"The Donora Geomancy," *Poet Lore*
"The Great Chain of Being," *The Missouri Review*
"The REM Sleep of Birds," *Poetry*
"Why We Care about Quarks," *The Kenyon Review*
"Forecasting the Dragon," *The Missouri Review*
"The Hunza Dream," *Poetry*
"Calculating Pi," *New England Review*
"The Universal Language of Waiting," *The Literary Review*
"The Air of Delicate Pastry," *Zone 3*
"Class A, Salem, the Rookie League," *The Gettysburg Review*
"The Local Cemetery," *Poetry*
"Enlisting," *Poetry*

### Writing Letters for the Blind

"Dragging the Forest," *North American Review*
"The Busy Darkness," *American Scholar/Oxford*
"The Fathers I Could See from My Room," *Witness*
"Marking the Body," *The Southern Review*
"What Color Did," *Poetry*
"The Early History of the Submarine," *The Paris Review*
"Otherwise Healthy," *Mid-American Review*
"The Plagues in Order," *Smartish Pace*
"Birds-of-Paradise," *North American Review*
"The Magpie Evening: A Prayer," *Prairie Schooner*

### Standing Around the Heart

"Standing Around the Heart," *The Paris Review*
"The Eternal Language of the Hands," *The Paris Review*
"Sweet Things," *DoubleTake*
"The Buchinger Limbs," *The Southern Review*
"The Uses of Rain," *The Missouri Review*
"Bringing Back the Bones," *The Georgia Review*
"The History of Silk," *Western Humanities Review*
"Anniversary," *The Southern Review*
"The Weaknesses of the Mouth," *The Southern Review*
"Headcheese, Liverwurst, a List of Loaves," *The Gettysburg Review*
"Coughing Through the Brambles," *The Missouri Review*
"Miss Hartung Teaches Us the Importance of Fruit," *The Paris Review*
"Johnny Weismuller Learns the Tarzan Yell," *The Paris Review*
"The History of SAC," *Boulevard*
"In Films, the Army Ants Are Always Intelligent," *Poetry Northwest*

### The Fire Landscape

"The Anomaly Museum," *The Gettysburg Review*
"Black Veils," *Prairie Schooner*
"The Sorrows," *Southern Poetry Review*
"The Horns of Guy Lombardo," *Prairie Schooner*
"False Dawn," *Michigan Quarterly Review*
"White Gloves," *Prairie Schooner*
"The Pause in the Plummet for Prayer," *Gettysburg Review*
"The 1918 House," *The Gettysburg Review*

### Reviving the Dead

"Telling the Bees," *The Southern Review*
"Dust," *Valparaiso Poetry Review*
"The Beheaded," *Alaska Quarterly Review*
"Evaluation," *Chariton Review*
"For Good," *Hampden-Sydney Review*
"Scattering," *Prairie Schooner*
"Translating the Hawk," *Prairie Schooner*

### The History of Permanence

"The Serious Surprise of Sorrow," *Alaska Quarterly Review*
"After the Aberfan Disaster," *Gettysburg Review*
"The Possibilities for Wings," *Virginia Quarterly Review*
"Selflessness," *Virginia Quarterly Review*
"The Dead Girls," *Ploughshares*
"Things That Fall from the Sky," *Beloit Poetry Journal*
"Something to Think About," *Gettysburg Review*
"Specificity," *Gettysburg Review*

### After the Three-Moon Era

"Calculations: A Love Poem," *New England Review*
"Reports," *Prairie Schooner*
"After the Three-Moon Era," *The Southern Review*
"Strangers, Falling," *The Gettysburg Review*
"According to Ibid," *The Southern Review*
"The History of Fail-Safe," *Green Mountains Review*
"The Illiterate in New Mexico," *Alaska Quarterly Review*

*The Infinity Room*

"Distraction Therapy," *Prairie Schooner*
"During the Retirement Semester," *The Gettysburg Review*
"Shadowing the Gravedigger," *The Southern Review*
"Assessing the Dead," *Valparaiso Poetry Review*
"The Startling Language of Shriveling Leaves," *Prairie Schooner*
"The Secret City," *American Journal of Poetry*
"Stunned," *100 Word Story*
"Worship," *Seminary Ridge Review*
"The Lengthening Radius for Hate," *Cervena Barva Press*
"The Chernobyl Swallows," *The Somerville Times*
"Anniversary," *Paterson Literary Review*

*The Mussolini Diaries*

"Fimbulwinter," *The Gettysburg Review*
"After the Election," *Lake Effect*
"Symmetry," *The Southern Review*
"Isolation," *World Literature Today*
"The Past Tense of the Census," *On the Seawall*
"Sparklers," *The Laurel Review*
"Contagious," *Gargoyle*
"Hole in the Head: A Love Poem," *Barrow Street*

*For Now, We Have Been Spared*

"The Art of Moulage," *Ploughshares*
"After War News," *Vox Populi*
"On the Death of Sons: An Elegy," *Live Encounters*
"My Daughter, Talking about Boys," *Alaska Quarterly Review*
"Choosing a Trail," *The Gettysburg Review*
"Unmoored," *Live Encounters*
"On the Eve of the Presidential Election," *St. Ann's Review*
"Advent," *Valparaiso Poetry Review*
"Pentecostal," *Brilliant Flash Fiction*
"Walking Backwards," *I-70 Review*
"Missing: A Psalm," *The Southern Review*
"The Unicorn Lair," *Salamander*

## Contents

### *The Days of Uncertain Health* (1988)

| | |
|---|---|
| The Girl Who Breathes Through a Hole in Her Throat | 3 |
| Quagmire | 4 |
| Street Cleaning | 5 |

### *Plant Voices* (1991)

| | |
|---|---|
| What the Builders Left | 9 |
| Groaning Boards | 10 |
| Sleeping with the Leper | 12 |
| Bourbon, Red Meat, Salt, Grease | 18 |
| Ants | 19 |

### *The Double Negatives of the Living* (1992)

| | |
|---|---|
| Naming the Sky | 23 |
| The Flower Remedies | 24 |
| The Stuttering Cures | 26 |
| Reaching the Deaf | 28 |
| Pet Cemetery | 30 |
| Six Kinds of Music, the Wallpaper of Breasts | 32 |
| The Double Negatives of the Living | 34 |

### *Inventing Angels* (1994)

| | |
|---|---|
| A Murder of Crows | 39 |
| The Book of Numbers | 40 |
| The Wonder Children | 42 |
| The Butterfly Effect | 44 |
| The Skill of the Sunlight's Good | 46 |
| Every Reachable Feather | 47 |
| Inventing Angels | 48 |

### *The Technology of Paradise* (1998)

| | |
|---|---|
| Hanging the Pigs | 53 |
| The Cabinet of Wonders | 54 |
| The Doctrine of Signatures | 56 |

*The Almanac for Desire* (2000)

| | |
|---|---|
| The Dark Angels | 59 |
| The Holy Numbers | 60 |
| The Natural Method for Dog Training | 62 |
| Schmaltz | 77 |
| The Terrors | 78 |
| The Spiritualists | 79 |
| Light Enough to Be Lifted | 80 |

*Blood Ties* (2002)

| | |
|---|---|
| The Tentative Steps of the Obese | 83 |
| The Extrapolation Dreams | 85 |
| The Donora Geomancy | 92 |
| The Great Chain of Being | 94 |
| The REM Sleep of Birds | 108 |
| Why We Care about Quarks | 109 |
| Forecasting the Dragon | 110 |
| The Hunza Dream | 112 |
| Calculating Pi | 114 |
| The Universal Language of Waiting | 115 |
| The Air of Delicate Pastry | 116 |
| Class A, Salem, The Rookie League | 118 |
| The Local Cemetery | 120 |
| Enlisting | 122 |

*Writing Letters for the Blind* (2003)

| | |
|---|---|
| Dragging the Forest | 125 |
| The Busy Darkness | 126 |
| The Fathers I Could See from My Room | 133 |
| What Color Did | 134 |
| Marking the Body | 136 |
| The Early History of the Submarine | 137 |
| Otherwise Healthy | 138 |
| The Plagues in Order | 139 |
| Birds-of-Paradise | 140 |
| The Magpie Evening: A Prayer | 142 |

*Standing Around the Heart* (2005)

| | |
|---|---|
| Standing Around the Heart | 145 |
| The Eternal Language of the Hands | 146 |
| The Buchinger Limbs | 147 |
| The Uses of Rain | 148 |
| Sweet Things | 149 |
| Bringing Back the Bones | 150 |
| Anniversary | 151 |
| The Weaknesses of the Mouth | 152 |
| The History of Silk | 153 |
| Headcheese, Liverwurst, a List of Loaves | 154 |
| Coughing Through the Brambles | 156 |
| Miss Hartung Teaches Us the Importance of Fruit | 158 |
| Johnny Weismuller Learns the Tarzan Yell | 159 |
| The History of SAC | 160 |
| In Films, the Army Ants Are Always Intelligent | 162 |

**The Fire Landscape** (2008)

| | |
|---|---|
| The Anomaly Museum | 167 |
| Black Veils | 169 |
| The Sorrows | 170 |
| The Horns of Guy Lombardo | 172 |
| False Dawn | 174 |
| White Gloves | 175 |
| The 1918 House | 176 |
| The Pause in the Plummet for Prayer | 178 |

**Reviving the Dead** *(2011)*

| | |
|---|---|
| Telling the Bees | 181 |
| Dust | 182 |
| The Beheaded | 183 |
| Evaluation | 185 |
| For Good | 186 |
| Scattering | 187 |
| Translating the Hawk | 189 |

## *The History of Permanence* (2011)

| | |
|---|---|
| The Possibilities for Wings | 193 |
| The Serious Surprise of Sorrow | 194 |
| After the Aberfan Disaster | 196 |
| Selflessness | 198 |
| The Dead Girls | 199 |
| Things That Fall from the Sky | 202 |
| Something to Think About | 208 |
| Specificity | 218 |

## *After the Three-Moon Era* (2015)

| | |
|---|---|
| Calculations: A Love Poem | 223 |
| Reports | 224 |
| After the Three-Moon Era | 226 |
| Strangers, Falling | 233 |
| According to *Ibid* | 234 |
| The History of Fail-Safe | 235 |
| The Illiterate in New Mexico | 237 |

## *The Infinity Room* (2018)

| | |
|---|---|
| Distraction Therapy | 241 |
| During the Retirement Semester | 242 |
| The Earth, We're Told, Is Humming | 244 |
| Shadowing the Gravedigger | 246 |
| Assessing the Dead | 248 |
| The Startling Language of Shriveling Leaves | 250 |
| The Secret City | 251 |
| Stunned | 260 |
| Worship | 261 |
| The Lengthening Radius for Hate | 263 |
| The Chernobyl Swallows | 274 |
| Anniversary | 275 |

*The Mussolini Diaries* (2020)

| | |
|---|---|
| Fimbulwinter | 279 |
| After the Election, Traditional Forms | 280 |
| Symmetry | 281 |
| Isolation | 282 |
| The Past Tense of the Census | 284 |
| Sparklers | 286 |
| Contagious | 288 |
| Hole in the Head: A Love Poem | 299 |

*For Now, We Have Been Spared* (2025)

| | |
|---|---|
| The Art of Moulage | 305 |
| After War News | 306 |
| Upon the Death of Sons: An Elegy | 309 |
| My Daughter, Talking about Boys | 317 |
| Choosing a Trail | 319 |
| Unmoored | 321 |
| On the Eve of the Presidential Election | 323 |
| Advent | 325 |
| Pentecostal | 327 |
| Walking Backwards | 328 |
| Missing: A Psalm | 330 |
| The Unicorn Lair | 332 |

Author Biography     337

*The Days of Uncertain Health* (1988)

# The Girl Who Breathes Through a Hole in Her Throat

The girl who breathes through a hole in her throat
Fills the library with mortality.
She makes us turn, keeps us from our reading;
She is the only one who concentrates.
Her deep breaths make us listen to our hearts,
Our breathing shallow as she approaches
Like the stalking skeleton with the scythe
We see in holiday weekend papers.
We are not on the bleak highway, yet feel
Control slipping away. If there were a pole
Or an oncoming car, we would hit it.
She reads, perhaps no longer hears herself.
It is a blessing we are not sharing.
The readers in this room are fast thinning.
This town will soon grow ignorant, and she
Will be left well read, a dread genius
In our midst reciting as she passes.

# Quagmire

Outside of town, the soft bog
Digests those things that die there.
We test it with our shoes, imagine
Hands upraised and the lungs filled,
The body deep brown like the emblem
Of a sinking, strangled country.

Our nervous dog knew someone, perhaps,
Who foundered here like those mammoths
And sharp-fanged tigers on multiple
Museum walls. In this quagmire, smother
Is a sign of spring; summer tempts us
To dig for our original selves, the bones
And weapons lost under our cautious feet.

Soon something may surface. The swamp,
A local farmer tells us, is spreading,
Bleeding out from this black wound.
Our house is downhill from here;
The Earth may be tipping. Some night,
After a March thaw, we will hear
The gurgling of a million lost voices
Thick with slime. Slipping under the door,
They will bubble and multiply, rising,
Like ancestry, toward a common ceiling.

# Street Cleaning

I have been thinking of the woman
Who died before we moved here, her cough
Coloring with pain through the fall:

That first night we slept on the floor,
Our furniture in New Jersey.
My throat went out again, my voice
Unnoticed along the curb where cars
Were positioned like confirmation
Of rumors. Before dawn, the haunting
Of our street began. The husband
In the house is dismantling hope;
The children have colds; a neighboring
Village is chronically burning.

It is the woman who died before we moved here.
It is the woman who watched the sun turn wound-red,
Tear, like flesh, near the horizon. And we are
Waiting across the street, unsure of dawn,
Paper birds circling our son's crib.

We eat her pickles, the woman who died before we moved here.
The children tease the sleeping ants with crumbs. About ten o'clock,
The factory unsubtle, black smoke pours over the town.
There is no remedy. Sloshing through
The pre-Christmas snow, we notice
The fine-ground pepper fallout, the off-white
Of something not quite certain: a fault, a crack
In the lungs opening like a miserable seam in our clothing.

In this town, the streets are regularly cleaned,
The science-fiction sucking sound outside
Our window at three, at four; things disposed of,
Gone into autopsy like unexpected deaths.

*Plant Voices* (1991)

# What the Builders Left

Some of them must have believed in symbols,
Leaving the refuse shaped just so, aligned
In arrows, pentangles, double daggers,
And one cross out back in the bulldozed mud
I'll be raking in April. Among them
Is a shale monolith stuck so upright
That no one would think *accident,* and I
Warn my children, "Stay clear," while I study
The folklore threats of East Snyder County,
How these fifth generation Germans pass
Hatred through their tales, how page after page
Of phone-book cousins say hemophilia,
Albino, and why did you relocate
Where builders make the time to form totems.
Someone named Kratzer restacked the lumber
In my living room; someone named Mengel
Snipped the wiring and bent it until fear
Drove sparks from mouth to tail. And whichever
Dunkleberger jammed this six-foot shale spear
Into this February mud, must have
Shouted for help, must have wig-wagged his arms
In a convincing way to bring at least
Two simple cousins who were uneasy
With touching this hex there is no chant for.

## Groaning Boards

In the Letters Section, the fundamentalists
Are talking about creation, how most readers'
Futures are fire. They're condensing antiquity,
Editing to verify Eden, and claiming
Carbon dating one more pitchfork brand on the soul.
"It's their diet," a friend laughs, handing me a plate,
His church-picnic food line so slow I examine
The broken barn across the highway, start thinking,
To pass time, I might witness its collapse into
One of those rubble piles you pass, anonymous
As all of these covered dishes, three-bean salads,
Scalloped potatoes, nothing noted until someone
Claims it's wood from an ark—Noah's, the Covenant's.
And I remember standing in these picnic lines
With plates as empty, searching for something to end
The embarrassment of taste. The congregation
Heaped coleslaw and baked beans, meat loaf and sauerkraut,
Macaroni, red-beet eggs, joking, "It all goes
To the same place." It was the Lord's plenty; it was
America's riches incarnate while the coal
Trains' schedules thinned into broth, the mines sewn back up
And sealed like cancer patients. Nobody mentioned
Subsidence, though the road to those picnics was roped
By the varicose veins of tipped houses. I found
Applesauce, ham it took seven minutes to trim,
And watched the old women stand like Joe Palooka
Air bags, catch themselves with weight through their thighs, and raise
Their canes and walkers like weapons. They admonished
Their bodies like Kathryn Kuhlman broadcasts: "Heal me,
Lord, though I'm not worthy," they whispered, eighty years
Of hauling the fat of the land on their shoulders.
The lard coating of the past on their tongues, first formed
By German, brought up the phlegm of repetitive
Work with its old-world cough of consonants. And here,

In Selinsgrove, it's God's Holiness Campground, horse
And buggy, the three hitching posts at Weis Market,
The translucent skull caps on two of the tellers
At Snyder County Trust, and one shrunken woman
At this feast who's dieting a tumor away,
Eating dried fruit and nuts to outlive her doctor.
She's up front with this year's examples; she's shaking
The golf ball out of her brain. When, some nights, I dream
Myself dead over cliffs, beside terrorist bombs,
In front of madman's shotguns, the next scene is black.
I keep it to myself like fear of failure, but
This traditional food speaks from the long tables,
Insists on God as I joke with my friend who loads
His plate for both of us, fat and laughing about
My nostalgic Pittsburgh beer, about his cabbage
Soup diet abandoned after diarrhea.
And I remember, too, that some of those women
Were tied to chairs, nodded and swayed through those Sundays'
Second sermons, that I wandered, afterward, through
The faithful like an erosion gulley, feeling
The fish-barb snag of guilt hook my shirt from behind.
And likewise, after we eat, in that barn's darkness,
My bored sons will grow quiet, paying attention
To a footfall of wind, retribution, using
Their sudden, bullhorn voices for balance, courage;
And in those groves at dusk, the oldest women would
Test themselves before waiting for hands to lift them.
All of those widows with humps would put prayer away
And limp to taxis driven by sons or nephews.
They believed wings could be latent in the spine's pain,
Patient as wisdom teeth, as breasts or beard or birth,
The rest of the body's redeemable promise.

## Sleeping with the Leper

*The Spider Behind Glass*

Our heartbeats. We talk ourselves
Awake and listen to nothing
As we shrivel. The spider
Behind glass has opened his home.

We gather each shred of light.
Our room is rearranged until
The untouched dust of neglect
Is positioned for our feet.

We ought to move, percentages
Still with us. So slowly, we
Push ourselves up on elbows,
Concentrate on the padded risks
That are not entirely silent.

Remember, this is no insect.
There are eight ways to hears its
Eraser shuffle. We swallow
The syllables that rise, each
Nerve listening for evidence.

*Centralia*

Some places transform air
Into ash, every protest
Burned when it touches down.
Which is what 1000 degrees does,
These hot spots that glow
In the night drizzle.
We watch them the way
We inspect our fireplace
Before sleep. One ember
May sputter to the carpet
Like lottery-luck.
We buy no tickets;

We are boarding up worry;
We are overlooking
The row house connection
Of our arson-prone lives.

That's our neighborhood
Testing our walls. At Park
And Locust, the cellar
Collapsed like a feeble coup,
All we see of politics.

That's the present metered
On our alarm: thirty-five parts
Per million sends a siren
Into our sleep because
We live over exhaust,
Because the hole for the hose
Shifts whenever whim grows bored.

Our canaries flutter
Like apprehension. Nothing
Is sustained but cures:
How someone will shrink
Our tumors into power;
How he will heat our homes
For 1000 years because
Niagara Falls tumbles
Underfoot . . .

December thins into
Our twenty-third year
Of this. Seen from above,
This constellation we
Walk on adds more detail,
Domestic animal feeding.

*The Field of Hot Spots*

"One of us would steal a newspaper from a porch and we'd run back into the field of hot spots, crumpling the paper into basketball wads we'd shoot—jump hooks, three pointers from way outside—checking our scores off each time our pages would take flame when they landed, though we got too good and one afternoon Joey Augustine hit seven in a row from twenty feet, exploding a whole Sunday financial section so fast we got bored and just balled up the rest of what we had and heaved it. We gave it up after that, remembering that last quick whoosh from four loose sections at once, something there is no sense doing again."

*The Movers*

We have come back to a house
In Centralia, its body
Boarded and locked, and we have
Come for the last time, loading
The things we have lived without.
They are heavy with weather,
Slush and smoke, the backyard vent
Shaping our share of the fire
Into a column. We are
Not speaking though we are words
Leaving the oil that burns
Inside rain, but we have come
Back to fill ourselves part-way
And be satisfied though we
Will dry before dark, tables
And beds behind us in trucks.
As flammable as our land,
As breathless as our basement,
We gut this house slowly and
Retreat to the road, driving
The detour until the first
Fissure yawns in our red past.

*Claude Wertz*

"This is a town where every liquor store box is hauled off to be packed with clothes, dishes, books. My father has taken up shouting; my mother has taken to church. Which makes me sneer, both of them, because Art Rooker talks of rifles each time a commission examines us. He says, 'We should empty each body of words,' and yesterday I learned the paragraphs of Shirley Weaver's life when her story ran in the paper after her monoxide alarm malfunctioned: I learned her neighbors joked about 'Shirley's Schoolhouse' because of the frequent bells; I learned anger was nothing like one of those fist-fights with some local jerk. The manufacturer's explanation ran down the column beside Shirley's picture until it turned to blood."

*The Tourists*

Now Route 61 has cracked
And these dry geyser
Steam clouds do not subtract
Vision in a dream of faults.
Now the soap smooth voice
At the press conference
Washes itself and leaves
Before the village sinks,
An unlucky, oiled bird.

So we take a camera walk
And feel like poachers, think
Of the deer with the arrow
In its head that made
The paper last week, how,
Surrounded by fence, it shared
The West Aliquippa curse,
Backed up to Ohio by trains.

Look, we laughed about that island,
The necessary overpass, and half
The roads here are closed.
A winter of no snow
Squats over Pennsylvania
And refuses to go,
And we take pictures
And listen to the grocer say,
"Twenty-three years we've been
Sleeping with a leper.
Twenty-three years we've been
Waking up surprised
Our faces are falling off."
We nod and expect a toll gate,
Someone ringing a contagion bell.

*Art Rooker*

"He was drunk at his wife's funeral. He spoke aloud when he meant to whisper, and that night, glass in hand, he made me walk with him into this vented field. There was a kind of half-light we had grown used to, knowing that a mile away the clear sky would not surprise us, draped at one end as if that window were ragged and broken. This time, standing beside him as he scuffed the soil for footing, I thought the moon was searching for us, a weak-battery flashlight that could never make anything out for certain, and whoever was holding it would have to call out and give himself away, saying something stupid like 'Is that you?' or 'Who's there?' It could have been a couple of minutes that he took to get his feet in place, shifting in tiny increments like wrist wrestlers trying to get that slim advantage of leverage. The nearest pipe was ten yards away. Another one stood twenty yards off. It was like walking on a factory roof except you had to imagine the looking down to where men would be busy when the shift-change came. 'Right now,' he said, 'we're the opposite of Noah, standing here on the first piece of the earth to die.' I wished I had brought a bottle with me—I had nothing to do with my hands except stick them in my pockets."

*The Stayers*

We have begun to think like snakes,
Aware of how we touch the earth,
And the copperheads have taught us,
Dragging our fear through Centralia.

Uneven, this crust over fire.
We watch our shoes for the sinking
First sign of collapse, and the snakes
Inside us swim on the soil.

The copperheads speak of surface.
These refugees talk through winter,
Disregard their blood. Subsidence.
Monoxide. Venom. Everything

Is feeding our choice. We coil.
We watch the smoke-fissure highway
Conceal each cracked house's travel.
Below us the copperheads are
Thinking of coal, thinking of feet.

*Donny Knouse*

"Later, I told her, as we lay on the unnatural warm earth, that we were becoming a national anecdote, and her expression explained that she did not understand me. I let it pass, imagining I could hear the fire underneath the soil, watching for something to change on her face which was almost lit by the light that flared beneath us."

# Bourbon, Red Meat, Salt, Grease

"I've been running mornings," my friend says,
"Trying to break even with the bourbon
And the red meat." I swat whatever is biting
At twilight and hold the last beer I'm having
Because I stop at eight. "All that salt,"
He says. "All that grease. I give myself
An hour on the highway to sweat it out."

His neighbor is watching us. He's maybe seventy,
And he's not holding a drink or playing
A doo-wop tape. I check him for a hair shirt.
I don't believe my friend is saving one day
Of his life by running, but I say, "Listen
To those guys singing their hearts out,"
Meaning Jackie and the Starlites, who are
Only begging for Valerie to come back,
Not a reprieve from chest pain, another morning
To wake up thinking, "That's the last time."

## Ants

In 1952, at a family picnic, my aunt
Warned me not to sleep on the grass.
She said ants would crawl up my nose
And told the story of a woman she knew
With an anthill in her forehead, how
She'd slept outside and, unknowing,
Woken with ants in her sinuses.

I was ready to start second grade,
Old enough, you'd think, to disbelieve
Something, but I brushed myself
While I listened to the rest
Of that victim's problems: her operation
To clear a colony of ants that had settled
On a kind of satellite, accepting
Those tunnels as home. I stared down
And saw how the grass teemed, how there
Were nightmares of ants that would explore
My head and approve. My uncles sat down
To cards; my aunts started to make that grove
Look like we'd never been there, and
I kept walking and brushing myself
Like someone half-trained at putting out
Fire, refusing to drop and roll, but
Not running like a cindered fool.

*The Double Negatives of the Living* (1992)

# Naming the Sky

"There's my sky," my father says. I don't know
what he expects, answer, in his driveway,
"It's clear, all right," and idling in neutral,
Think he's planning to tell me the ancient
Names for the dots or the tales they fathered,
People who suffered, changed, and ascended
While somebody handed their stories down.
Two dippers and Orion—I forget
The rest or never learned or failed to see
Anything but the stars scattered on our scale
Of pulse and breath. I want him to show me
Archer, bear, lion; I want marble busts
Of myth to form above us like pillars
Of flame, chariots of fire, accounting
For every light, and because my mother
Has died, wonder if he means to show me
Where she is, how one cluster has reformed
To suggest a melodrama of hope.
Heavy-headed with travel, I wait while
The time-released light, set to eleven,
Blinks off in his living room like stars near
The horizon tumbling off the sky's screen.
And I remember no clock in this house
Is correct, all six set so fast no one
Would believe them, early as wet robins
In today's false thaw of February.
We stand with the night in our lungs; we breathe
A sentence of silence until he says,
"Venus and Jupiter," directs me low
In the sky where I see so many lights
I can nod, certain they are among them.

# The Flower Remedies

1
"Are flowers thinking?" my son asked once.
"Do they know who we are?" and I worried
For his manhood, wished he'd requested
A translation for snarls, the idioms
Of growls. "They know us like the newly born,"
I told him. "If they breathed, they would cry."

2
Nothing could keep Edward Bach from flowers.
Not scoffing. Not weather. Not the symptoms
He showed when he approached the proper plants:
Hatred near holly; beside mustard, gloom.
So sensitive, Bach was, he imagined
Self-pity by chicory; guilt at pine.
They healed him and cured the distress of those
Who drank his flower-teas. Take cerato
For self-doubt; taste iris for frustration;
Then smile, sip aspen for anxiety,
Whisper, "Bach," say, "The Flower Remedies."

3
I hear my wife say her student, today,
Sat up barking, and she thought, like her class,
He was joking, a first-day-of-school test
For his teacher. "He was growling," she says.
"He sounded so much a dog I thought it
Was talent." Under the table our Spitz
Lies listening to what it knows; already
I want to say "Well?" but my wife offers
The syndrome's name for bad luck in the genes.
Snarl, spit, what the old exorcists knew.
Our dog waits to sit and beg, but no one
Is holding food. The house-trick it's mastered—
Not to be deceived by one thing at least,
Thinking in barks and growls like a student.

4
To believe in the brain's
Many routes from disease;
To learn stress buffers;
To read this week's book
On meditation, stretching,
Deep breathing and joy.
"Rock rose for panic, gorse
For despair"—each day is
Pocked with moods; what we
Become has walked in others
And still we study. Choler,
We read—bile, phlegm, blood—
So medieval in another
Smug week of solutions.

5
I am walking to work, thinking of flowers. How few I recognize. The roadside is littered with mysteries, and I know as little about the cars that brush my walking. I need a lesson in America, in goods, in the names for constructed things, and I say, "Cerato, iris, aspen" to begin the multiplication of forgetfulness. I would turn into these fields if I remembered the identity clues—color, shape, pattern, number—everything leaves and petals, each of my terrors swept away by the undertow of flowers.

# The Stuttering Cures

One thing we learn: how much poison
The body can take. Alcohol,
For instance. Cruelty. Prayer as duty.
Once a day Ronnie Muller read
History aloud because Mrs. Cook
Demanded a paragraph
Of recitation. Stuttering's cure,
Perhaps, though Ronnie Muller,
Force-fed like a protest faster,
Never finished a sentence
Before P or T swallowed
His breath and the carburetor
In his throat stalled for good.
Always, there is worse, some surgeon
A hundred years before Mrs. Cook who
Snipped portions of stutterers' tongues,
Clipped strategic bits and pieces
Like speech therapy's barber.

All of those stories of stutterers
Who can sing, who can whisper,
Who can perfectly speak in unison
Or when they cannot hear themselves:
Each one of those patients, after
The plastic surgery for speech,
Waited for that doctor to unwrap
His transformed tongue, to say, "Yes, now,"
As welcome. Think of that first
Tentative stutter, the patient
Hearing imperfection's nuance,
The misery of misdirected breath
Lengthening to the wish for
The speechless life of stone.
So easily, the wind we've stored

Scatters the memos of our thinking.
The man who sold me insurance
Lost his tongue to cancer, entered
The enormous stammer of silence,
The messages on his note pad
Thinning to *yes* and *no*, to tapping,
At last, on the empty tablet,
Nothing anyone could decipher,
As if it were a personal code
Or all his thoughts now stuttered.

# Reaching the Deaf

> *Screams of distress are in the vocal spectrum least affected by age deterioration.*
> —*Extraordinary Endings*

I've cursed behind my mother,
Spent my rage-list of phrases
While she scrubbed grease from plates.
My father, now, hears nothing
On his right, and I've tested him
With blasphemy from the shotgun seat.
And I've settled, full front,
For vague heresies, measured
My lies by volume, but here is
The news of Gertrude Jameison,
Eighty-five, harassing
Doug Thompson forty-six years,
Calling him eight times a day
Despite court orders, four months
At a penal farm, and a lock
On her phone. Nothing's stopped her.
Not a stroke. Not confinement
In a nursing home. Not Thompson
Gone so silent on the line
She asks if he knows her, if he
Has something to say, shrill
With still guessing the phrase
To stop his heart. Some screams
Must run the painted needle to
The North of the penny compass.
Some distress must sing itself
Up the noon or midnight
Of the gumball clock. Think of
The way a woman calls and calls;
How another waters her lawn
All day for a year, swamping
Herself and her neighbors, what

She means to say in her faucet,
The sum of her language forming
A shrieking wetland. Think how
The pulse of imminence searches
Through things in common, speeding us to
The bestial vowels that reach the deaf.

## Pet Cemetery

It was the kind of place
I walked with a notebook,
A grant supporting me
Cross country. I copied
Down inscriptions that seemed
Parodies and wondered
What anyone driving
Route 80 would think of
Edgar Friedell paying
Somebody to inscribe
*Bambi Was My Baby*
On a headstone. I thought
Of how I was spending
Pennsylvania's money,
Believing I could find
Poems daily by starting
My car, remembering
The fat anthologies
I carried, the number
Of fellowship winners
Like myself who filled up
American highways
Until they found one place
That convinced them they were
Alone. I walked down past
*Our Lost Little Girlie*
And *My Sweetie* and stood
On the shoulder the way
I did before I thought
About poems or how much
One of those drivers could
Make me pay for a ride,
And I kept guessing how
I looked to every man

Or woman who might be
Watching for hitch-hikers,
And Christ, I wanted to
Heave that notebook across
The highway, one more tax
Dollar symbol, and I
Wanted Edgar Friedell
To show up with flowers
So I could ask him how
He'd done it, loved something
Enough to sign his name.

## Six Kinds of Music, the Wallpaper of Breasts

I thought I'd drive the seventy miles
To see my son, slouch in a dorm room
With six kinds of music, the pleasure
Of his wallpaper of breasts. His wild hair
Was jammed down his shirt; we said nothing while
We breathed together as he looked for shoes
And I thumbed through his college catalogue
As if it were *People* at the dentist.

I recognized Tom Petty, Prince, The Who.
I heard, when another door swung open,
The Fine Young Cannibals, and I could have
Asked my son who else was singing along
That hall, but he said, finally, "That guy
On the cover was arrested for rape."
I closed his core curriculum and looked
Again at the student in the sweatshirt,
The name of my son's school across his chest
To sell parents, because he was seated
In the stacks, a sense of scholarship.

I felt like the fool of the worthless deed,
The lunkhead of the nosedived junk bond.
That student's slick smile had beamed at us
Through a senior year of choices; I'd tried
To read the titles of the books bunched on
The shelf behind him and made jokes about
The fabricated pose of study, how
Two hundred catalogues we owned had been
Cloned like the white pillars, ivy, and
The quarter-hour chorus of carillons.

I wasn't sure what it meant to have
A rapist on that cover, see my son
In his sweatshirt across the lawn from
Where a new library was being built.
For all I knew, the girl lived in that dorm,
Had a copy of this catalogue
Among her books. "He's history," I heard.
"He's expelled." And one of the stereos,
At least, was softened, turned off, or the door
Of its owner's room was so unlikely
Thick it shut the sound inside like a hand
Insistent over an astonished mouth.

## The Double Negatives of the Living

After the pastor spoke well,
After he opened our route
With syntax and grammar
Correct as his manner,
I could follow my mother
To her grave and lapse into
The double negatives
Of the living. I could talk
Two hours past midnight with
My father in the steelworker
Idiom of his city, hearing
The fried mush of morning,
The white Sunday silence,
The many tongues of the cross
Speaking dialect stories
Of the holy mill. I could catch
His punctuation by breath born
In the thick ash of evening,
Overhear the end stops in
His coughs, the accidental case
For the thrift store's stock,
The body's swift tumors;
The chance of modifiers
For the factory uncles,
The fat, baking aunts,
The grandmothers in the pews
Of their dead husbands
Or rocking on porches
Flush with the brutal streets.
And finally, the commas for
Steel, rivers, bridges, bars.

And Christ, the Expletive,
And all of the language
Of the land that we leave
And return to, reopening
The earth and stammering
Like the past's twin-speech,
What we know by repeating,
What runs on without us.

*Inventing Angels* (1994)

# A Murder of Crows

Driving home, I see all of them
By the highway, pecking at
Whatever is splayed out and torn,
And none of them flutter up
Or hop deeper on the shoulder.
The houses start to thicken,
The one set back from the road owned
By a woman who has been
Moved upstate for care. At the light,
I turn slowly and hear nothing
Promising in the noise the brakes
Make, how they remind me they
Will eventually fail, but
The man who lives next door says
He has a book for me downstairs,
And I have to watch him limp
Toward the dark, thinking how little
I read. I could stammer that
Words are ineffective as skin,
But I follow him and see
His cellar ceiling-high with books.
"Seventy-thousand," he says,
Nodding at the fire-hazard piles
Of them. We smile together
Though the room is impassable,
And I know I will never
Open the volume he hands me,
*Vanity Fair*, his seventh
Garage-sale copy, and I could
Repeat, "A labor of mules,
A drift of hogs," tell him about
The collective nouns for things,
How names can amuse us and do
Nothing to change this evening,
Whether the weight of this novel
Impresses me or he will
Follow it with others, stacking
Them in my arms and never
Imagining I could drop them.

## The Book of Numbers

> *Using a standard typewriter, Marva Drew, from 1968 to 1974, typed the numbers from 1 to 1,000,000 on 2,500 pages.*
> —*The Best of the Worst*

Fat with ambition, this book,
Though you can see how its plot
Must progress regularly
As wills in the careful scripts
Of scriveners. In this tale,
Everything says conclusion.
Each symbol, each myth predicts
A sort of Rapture when life
Goes blank as an end page, all
Of the story well-planned as
An Earth-centered universe.
I want, tonight, to say I've
Started that book of numbers
So often I think it's mine.
At least to a thousand, where
I've stopped; or once, ten thousand,
A weekend with childhood flu,
My aunt hauling the pages
Downstairs to ponder. "You got
Every number right," she said,
Reporting like proofreaders.
Ten thousand and one, I thought,
Ten thousand and two, and went
Outside, after that fever,
To bounce a ball off the roof,
Off the wall, to simulate
One tense game in a season
Of one hundred-fifty-four.
And in ten years, if one group
Of believers is correct,
The world will explode because
That year matches the number

Of weeks Jesus walked the world.
The next year, too, will shatter
Us, a famous psychic claims,
And then the year 2000
Will send millions of hopefuls
Up the mountains to welcome
The universal blindness.
Thus, we need someone to count,
Take on a second volume
To insure we don't know how
It all turns out. "Pass it on,
No returns," we say, schoolboys
Punching the arms beside us.
Or circled, Boy Scouts, around
A campfire: "Jack still burning,"
Puffing on a glowing stick,
Handing it off before it
Goes black. One million and one,
Marva, one million and two . . .

## The Wonder Children

His parents posed beside him, the latest
Child prodigy, thirteen, is tonight's good news.
He's entering medical school, puberty,

And the reporter is pleased to predict,
To say many of us will be grateful
For the certainty of his surgeon's hands.

Doogie Howser, she tries, citing sitcom
As if it were history, counting on
Most of us to know her network's lineup,

Though she could mention a hundred children
Sure with scalpels, repeat Mozart, Mill,
And Henry Truman Safford. Or tell us

The Willy Sidis story, not optioned
To television, not yet—his entering
Harvard, eleven years old; his leaving

Learning behind, saying *no* to lectures
And libraries with a self-inflicted
Resignation. How he adopted the broom

And mop. How his hands welcomed the scythe,
Stacked the streetcar transfers he treasured.
How he died, forty-six, in a rented room,

Outliving a host of precocious children:
Cardiac, master of languages, dead
At seven; the Infant of Lubeck,

The Bible's index, expired at four, each
A wonder child forever like the one who
Mapped the only route to the needle's-eye

Entrance to heaven. Calculated the miles,
Established the angle of ascension.
And left the precise point of departure

For some future child genius to figure.
Including the rate of change for all things,
Their positions within the shifting sky

To one thousandth of a second as we
Revolve and spin, as each location in
The universe simultaneously moves.

Like our moon, we know, which is spiraling
Away from earth, and, in a million years,
Will be too distant to eclipse the sun.

## The Butterfly Effect

*If a butterfly flaps its wings in Brazil, it might produce a tornado in Texas.*
               —*The Laws of Chaos*

Early in the newsmagazine,
These Haitian women are wailing,
And those who are not are holding
Their breath and the hands of men
Tense with a bullet expectation.
And I've read, too, that the wind,
Tonight, may have originated
From their mourning, the beating
Of their arms in the air sending
This record warm front north.
I've read about fractals,
The Russian Dolls of the universe,
Diamonds made of diamonds made
Of diamonds diminishing in size;
I've learned the Butterfly Effect,
How chaos is not chaos,
How some slaughter in Haiti flaps
Its wings and churns into my grip
On the arm of my son, my clenched teeth
And hiss as he flutters his free arm
And wails and changes the future
Of weather in a country east of us
Where a father will choose, he thinks,
To stun his son to obedience.
And when I leave him to let the dog
Walk me into sense, the unnatural wind
Chatters the branches that skitter her
To a barking panic on our street

Of sculpted shrubbery where Christmas bulbs,
In one yard, might be arranged
Into language if you're properly
Angled, upstairs, across the street,
Positioned like an antenna straining
For a distant station, my son in his window
Watching me handle the dog, my breath
Without its winter clouds, nothing he'd believe
Could join the southern grief of a warm front.

# The Skill of the Sunlight's Good

The miracle animals approach, creep
Forward like the Ugandan Tortoise,
Who talked from his shell, or leap
Like Chris, the Psychic Dog, barking
Futures. They nod, paw, tap hooves—
And Lady Wonder, the Telepathic Horse,
Put her nose on oversize keys to print
Fortunes. What typos to hunt and peck;
She nudged and pressed, prophecy if you
Bought "The Skull of the Sinlight's Goof."
She could have been an economist,
Could have run for office and dictated
Letters to secretaries hired to follow
The mute inflections of her grammar.

Which of us scoffs? We won't harm anyone
With an ESP for heaven, mouthing hymns,
Chanting phrases of faith. There were weeks
I memorized Bible verses, recited them
At the altar, and I wasn't crippled.
This week I've sung "The Old Rugged Cross"
And repeated the standard prayer
Of the church aloud. And in public.
After I said "Amen," a child I'd known
Was off to burial. So be it.
So the animals use four legs forward
And do wonderful things if we let
Our mouths open to the old words of snort
And bark and nicker, saying, "Of course."

# Every Reachable Feather

On Sundays, now, my youngest son completes
His confirmation schooling, has me check
The answers for his Bible-study homework:

Besides Jesus, who rose from the dead?
He's written Lazarus like the workbook
Wants, but I suggest figurative Jonah,

The fortunate falls of Adam and Eve,
Confusing my son and recalling
How a neighbor, dead this week, hated

His wife's parrot for its squawking echo.
Look at my snake, he'd say. Never a noise.
Hardly a mess. And he set that boa

Loose to coil around the parrot's cage.
That quiets it, he'd say, and finally
The parrot went mute, his wife complaining

It was crazy, that parrots who utter
Nothing are depressed, and I agreed
Because every reachable feather

Was gone. If it had hands, she told me,
It would have plucked its head, and I said,
"It looks like food," just before my neighbor

Wrapped his fat arms around the cage, pressed
His face to the bars as if he didn't
Fear for his eyes. There was madness,

The constrictor coiling as it must,
The parrot suffocating in the dark,
Reviving, reviving again,

A home-bound record for resurrection,
Plucked and crazed and skittering back to
The vacant eternity of owners.

## Inventing Angels

1
Let us explain, the church said, the mystery
Of the inexplicable bones. One: God ran tests,
What did we think? There's always waste—to get
Eden right, He had to fail a thousand times,
All those bones the rejected prototypes
For paradise. Two: God, for personal
Reasons, don't ask, created fossils. Wouldn't
You use omniscience for deceit? Wouldn't
You test your people with the illusion
Of previous life? Three: There were species
Too late for the ark, the animals at fault,
Indifferent to "All aboard." A pair
Of mammoths dawdled; the pterodactyls waffled;
Noah had enough to do with rationing,
With teaching the Peaceable Kingdom precepts.

2
Or Noah, we guessed, senses that ark too small.
Afraid to blame God for the stupid specs,
He discreetly left half the world behind.
On Sundays, we learned the revised standard
Version of his story from a flannel board.
We followed felt cutouts through Noah's journey;
We heard reports on each Ararat attempt,
The church or celebrities funding those climbs
For the ark's splinters on the favorite
Mountain of the faithful. And we imagined
That cloth reshaped to everything preserved
By lava or tar whenever our teacher
Fast-forwarded to old Abraham and
The near-sacrifice he made following
The next audible orders from God.

3
The aurochs, quagga, great auk, and moa—
In the heresy of the backward glance,
An astonishment of passenger pigeons
Blackens the sky. One bird, its eyes sewn shut,
Is tied by hunters to a stool. And it calls
Loudly, of course, from the dark, drawing the flock
To the pogrom until nothing remains
But gangsters' slang, how we've used the dodo,
Which posed for artists, stood still for butchers,
The intent of predators bred from its genes.
What lasts? What Lasts? A hundred years after
It disappeared, the flightless dodo turned
To hoax: Because there were no skeletons.
Because portrait art was weak evidence
Against the circumstantial disbelief.

4
The immediate doubt of the witness—
In each museum, we read to verify
The bones, even those with hides or feathers
Like Martha, the last passenger pigeon,
Who was caged in the Cincinnati Zoo,
Who died and was not buried and rose again
As exhibit a year after Moreschi,
The last *castrato*, retired. The labels
On each of his ten recordings call him
The Soprano of the Sistine Chapel,
The church confessing to the altered truth
Of its soloists, inventing angels
We can visualize by listening
To the museum's gramophone, rapt with hearing
The pure, unnatural voice of extinction.

*The Technology of Paradise* (1998)

# Hanging the Pigs

*During the middle ages, there were dozens
of murder trials against animals.*

For murder, it was always
The domesticated, pigs
Especially, the ones who
Trampled children, danced their hooves
Through memory's red seizure.

Or the pigs, sometimes, were tortured,
Squealed clear confessions of guilt.
And locked in solitary,
They grunted the black mass prayer,
Snuffled to the devil's sleep,
So closely guarded, so bound,
None of those killers escaped.

And when they trotted, back-whipped,
To trial, a few of those pigs,
According to the records,
Had court-appointed lawyers
To plead the victim-defense,
The mental-deficiency
Gambit, none of it moving
The men who stood in for God.

So all were executed—
Hammered, butchered—and some led
To the gallows, snouts sliced off,
Wearing white human masks, dressed
In coats and trousers, lifted
To the bleating, back-legged stance
Of the hell-Pentecost, all
The silenced crowd pressed forward,
Waiting for those pigs to hang,
Shutting up their Satan tongues.

## The Cabinet of Wonders

> *Frederick Ruysch, the great embalmer, could fill all the veins
> and arteries, none ruptured, before his solution hardened.*
> —Finders, Keepers

Such expertise, Ruysch gained, at perfecting
Preservation, he worked with capillaries,
With filling the fine vessels of the face
So well these infants' heads in bottles float
Eyes open, as if surface still mattered.
Here, in this jar, an arm rising from lace
To grip an eye socket centuries old.
Here, a skull vented for a view of the brain.
Here, the small skeleton that holds a mayfly
To remind us of transience those mornings
When the *wunderkammer* of sickness takes
All the available space with the keepsakes
Of pain, the curios for fever, and
The repeated mementoes of wheezing.

In this museum in which we love ourselves,
The dispassionate fetus will not break
Its stare. Severed at the neck, we know, yet
Ruysch's daughter sewed the lace for its throat,
Selected beads; and sometimes she helped him clothe
His allegorical tableaux, fetal
Skeletons walking and weeping and playing
The violin with a dried-artery bow.

Geology of kidney stones, botany
Of blood vessels and lungs, intestine snakes
(Though the wonder is we need these warnings)
Which slither up from the fields to wrap these bones—
I've listened to "possible mass" after
One of those landscape kidney stones doubled
Me down to emergency. I've posed for
Tableaux with CAT-Scan and seen myself exposed

On the bulletin board for death, so many
Patients waiting in those subdivided rooms
We could have formed our own tableaux for fear,
A full *kunstkammer* where the conditions
Of our bodies could have been curated
To display the memory absolutions.

Whatever Ruysch is saying now, these rooms are
Weaving me inside. In the hypothesis
Of the Stendahl Syndrome, some tourists grow
Giddy after art. Their pulse accelerates.
They sweat and faint, or hallucinate, some
Of them depressed, some euphoric, some of them
Omnipotent in their hearts, though so many
Of these displays have been lost I can only
Trace the outline of every suspect organ
I can locate, running my fingers along
The perimeter of the liver to feel
For exactly what I never want to find.
Although as soon as I think this, I say
Of course not, how silly, like the doctor
Who, when I insisted I could distinguish
One kidney heavier than the other,
Shook his head sadly and said "impossible."

# The Doctrine of Signatures

The woman who followed me from flower
To flower said Birthday? Anniversary?
And I shook my head among the arrangements
Until she shifted to Accident? Sickness?
Guiding and pointing and introducing
The Doctrine of Signatures, how all plants
Were created to serve us, their powers
To cure revealed by shape, by size, by shade:
The bloodshot blossoms of the eyebright
Heal pinkeye; the Chinese lantern plant
Is bladder-shaped for stones. Paracelsus,
She said, acknowledging the source, adding
Yellow plants for the liver, ginseng root
For general malaise, prescriptions
So simple we could arrange eternity
In a greenhouse if we knew the shapes
Of our weakest parts, my mother's heart
Winding down while I thought of petals
Red and sugared as a lover's gift.
And since then I've comparison-shopped
For pancreas, thyroid, lymph glands, walking
The aisles with such ignorance of form
I might as well choose a shape for the soul—
Lilac, lily, morning glory—as if
Resurrection could be watered and fed
While we search for the flowers which form
Like tumors, the buds which open into
The ominous mass on the x-ray,
And the seeds or spores that are scattered
Like great seasonings for the earth, blended
So perfectly they lie invisible
Until they rise from our astonished tongues.

*The Almanac for Desire* (2000)

# The Dark Angels

To the sidewalk in front of my father's
Razed bakery I return. To the patch
Of burdock where the stacked ovens deep-browned
The crusts of a million loaves and rolls.
To the cinderblock cracked like the soot-pocked
Windows where I watched, in Etna, the dark
Angels escape the coal smoke as if they
Wanted to swoop back to chimneys. To shards
And splinters where I hated the sauerkraut
In the cramped, next-door kitchen, the boiled
Shank end of pork that clustered flies against
The latched screen door. To the steep, shale downslope
Where the walls of the bakery are landfill,
Where the first bulldozed soil coats wallboard
And lumber as if coal were refueling
Industry's return, covering the spot
Where I was careless, once, with Saturday's
Trash fire. Where it followed the easy weeds
To the brittle boards of the bakery.
Where the neighbor shook free the flies and sprayed
His hose and a set of obscenities
Keyed to my foolish name. Where my father
Thanked him and led me to the last eclair,
Settled me on the work room's folding chair
And said nothing except "think," and I thought
That neighbor was listening at the window
While I held chocolate and custard until
My father said, "You eat that," and I did.

# The Holy Numbers

We listened, as always, to Pastor Dave,
learning the Bible's major numbers, one
through the nine sixty-nine of Methuselah,
who lived eight times longer than all of us
put together. We memorized the three
parts of the Trinity, the four Gospels.
We recited the Ten Commandments
and the names of the twelve disciples,
subtracting Judas the Betrayer
before we matched them to the eleven
of ourselves, the future fishers of men.
Pastor Dave told us sacrifice stories,
the number of ways to be crucified,
including upside down, but the five boys
wanted to know the number of minutes
Jesus lasted on the cross, the number
of stones it took to slaughter Stephen.
Pastor Dave made us recite the Nicene
and the Apostles Creed, listening for
lapses because we were the future
of a faith that could spout, in unison,
the sixty-six books of the Bible,
ending with Revelation and its lists
of sevens and twelves. And I wanted
to ask the number of men who'd taken
Mary Magdalene to bed, and how much
she charged. And not asking, I counted,
on my own, the years I had until
three score and ten, learned the date for Easter
in 2015, when I needed
to rise from the dead and be repaid
for the 10% I'd been taxed by God.

Because I didn't see myself among
the nine groups blessed by Beatitudes,
not the boys who were poor in spirit;
not the meek we taunted; not the six girls
who were pure in heart, their bodies numbered
by breasts and thighs when the boys picked partners,
choosing until one was unchosen,
becoming the Virgin Mary, shifting
in her chair as if she were already
counting the two major heart attacks
of Pastor Dave, the three weeks between them,
the forty-two years he lived, including
the twenty-seven days after he laid
his hands to our heads and declared us saved.

# The Natural Method for Dog Training

*Torture, which was once a craft, has become a technology.*
                —Dr. Timothy Shallice

1
My mother said, "Accept no rides from strangers.
Don't even approach an unfamiliar car."
My father told me his search-party story,
The naked boy found, too late, tied to a tree.
The tongue was pulled from his throat; the lines still breathe.
"You never catch those drivers," my father said,
Yet I stood at the roadside, thumb extended,
And he swerved at me so suddenly I took
The guardrail with the step and leap of panic.

2
To teach, according to the slim manual
Called *The Natural Method for Dog Training*,
You lay tacks on the furniture, covering
The forbidden places for sleep. You throw
Firecrackers from your moving car to keep
That dog off the road. You spray it with a hose.
You place rat traps among the roses where
Digging's not allowed. And when nothing works,
You starve the animal to show who's boss.
It will come begging, then, apologetic
And compliant. You will own a well-trained dog.

3
When the General came to our school,
When he lectured us at the assembly
About the A-bomb and the safety
Of America, he called radiation
"Cloudshine" to honor the sky's pink glow.
One teacher, when the science fair
Arrived, told us a girl in Utah,
The year before, brought the head and neck
Of a cow for her exhibit, those parts
Split open to show the tumors
That had murdered her father's herd.
In another part of the country
A man hypothesized hormesis,
The therapy of low-level rads
To toughen us toward longer lives.
Pantywaist, sissy, mama's boy—
We were still using, to cure cowardice,
The old therapy of name calling.
Pansy, fairy, faggot, queer—
The double-dare of the schoolyard
And boot camp made it easier
To gut than go home, to shoot than say NO.
Trial and error. School of hard knocks.
We cry or don't cry. We grin and bear it
Or we scream and run. No pain, no gain,
Like the man whose leg cracked last night
When he lifted the most weight of his life.
We put our fingers to the flame;
We lay them on the coils just after
The red fades. So our lives will be better.
So we can distinguish right from wrong
And be numbered among the saved.

4
Once upon a time, doctors pulled the foreskin
Over the tip of the penis, punched holes
And stitched it to prevent masturbation.
That will do for now, they said to parents.
He'll think twice or pay the penalty
Of pain for allowing sin's tumescence.
There were remedies, from the beginning,
For every carnal crime, including
The natural method of castration,
So effective, so long, it was used
On epileptics and the insane.
Weren't seizures just sexual release?
Didn't the original sin of sex
Propel the weak to mental illness?
"The most significant factor
In social reform in history"—
What one expert declared just as
The era of the electric chair
Began, just as civilization was
About to be rid of capital crimes.

5
In the history of aversion therapy,
In the celebrated cases when cures
Were claimed, the physicians always speak.
Like Alexander Morrison, the champion
Of camphor oil, his patients swallowing
Their way to sweating and vomiting,
Diarrhea, convulsions. "That does it,"
He said, publishing his lectures to acclaim,
How he followed the progress of nine men
Who practiced "the crime against nature."
The way they took their dose with the sight
Of naked men. The way two of them changed,
Or so they said, cured of one kind
Of insanity. The way the lust
Of seven was so severe they stayed
Aroused, near-death, by anything male.
Like John Wesley, who ministered
With the electric friction machine
To save the worst of his Methodist flock.
"The unparalleled remedy," he said,
Preaching the gospel of therapy
As if it were one more metered phrase
For a hymn, the one in progress while
He watched the hair rise on the lunatics
Of little faith, those who might be rescued
From hell by small bolts of holiness,
Something like the practices of Saint Rose,
Who wore a chastity belt for life,
Throwing away the key. Who daily
Whipped herself. Who ate poisons, then fasted
Near death. Who disfigured herself. Who wore
A hair shirt and a crown of thorns. Who dragged
With her a wooden cross, preceding
St. Marina, not outdone, who added,
To her belt, spikes and iron teeth.

6
In one test, snails were fed a food
They'd never tasted, given two hours
Before sickened by injection.
Always, after that, they refused
That dinner, even weeks later,
A long stretch for the memories
Of snails. And surely the patients
Who vomit recall, outstripping
The snails, memorizing like birds
Who retrace their migration paths
Or die; like deer who recollect
The proper winter trails or starve.
In California, in the late Sixties,
In the state hospitals at Vacaville
And Atascadero, patients were
Softened by Anectine, overdosed,
With or without a medical release:
Complete paralysis, breathing stopped
For three minutes, subject still conscious,
The better to be conditioned by
The suggestions of the doctors.
"An extremely negative experience."
One witness said, yet those sex offenders,
Those criminally insane, were told,
When released, the do-it-yourself
Therapies of snapping rubber bands
Against their wrists, shoving fingers
Down their throats when unorthodox
Sex thoughts began. And, for tough cases,
The do-it-yourself of a shock machine
Made portable. "Useful in the playground"—
How the catalogue put it while I was
Busy with monkey bars and swings,
All that playground metal conducting

Improved behavior through my childish frame.
That did it, not the collective shock
Which worsened us, not the sad siren
Of civil defense, the tight tuck
In the stairwell, or the sprawl behind
The green dumpster when caught outside.
For improvement, you needed to be
Singled out, to cry where everyone
Could see you, every wail as visible
As a stain spreading from the crotch.

7
So late in December, so cold
across the full width of Ohio,
I was working up the self-pity
of "casualty," equating myself
with the sleepers on sidewalks.

So long between rides, I skipped
pre-scanning the driver to see
what he might charge, a policeman,
the car unmarked, or a man
in uniform aroused by boys.

I used classroom diction. I kept
eye contact with the highway,
the border five miles away. And when
we passed the welcome sign, not slowing,
I thought I was a sadist's dream.

In Pennsylvania, where I was
heading, a man had entered the homes
of women with a store-bought badge.
He let them live to be witnesses,
all six repeating boots and blue hat,
the dark-brown holster, none of them
remembering a face. "You know you're
illegal," he said, while I studied
chin and nose, a scar below the ear.
"If I choose," he said, "I'll make you pay."

Two days to the new year, that car
unheated to keep him up, I poured
the night sweats of the terminal.
He listed bus and train, the relative
safeties of ticketed rides.

Outside, ambiguous snow swirled up,
then cleared. He said he had pictures
of a boy flung into a landfill,
the work an overnight of rats
can do. He said, "Look under the seat"

and I didn't. He said, "End of the line,"
slowed, and the animals of evening
said nothing while I filled the door.
They might have been listening for
the sweet groans of dawn while he u-turned,

while he opened his window and drove
the soft shoulder like a mailman
to deliver a photograph
which brushed me, then fluttered between
his tire tracks, face down like choice.

8
Throughout high school, story after story
About radiation sickness, the short
And long term of it in Nevada
And Utah, testimonials from
Survivors about a smorgasbord
Of cancer and government denials.
And one story, finally, about
The benefits of uranium, how
It pulls diseases from the body,
Sending patients into played-out mines
For the cure of the abandoned cave.
And then a rush of precedents, including
The claims of Elisha Perkins,
Who held a patent on The Tractor,
Two rods which drew disease from the body
By the mix and alignment of alloys,
How they were held, lowered and raised
Like the palms of Christ or the surrogates
Who placed their healers' hands and prayed
At sunrise service, telling the tumors
To follow the sun. And there were
Testimonials, a neighbor's breast
Restored, an uncle's tumor shrunk.
And whether those old recoveries
Proved those rods responsible,
Whether cure lasted for hours or years,
George Washington, for one, believed,
Bringing his family to the early version
Of the uranium cure, though he was bled,
Just before death, by his doctors,
Submitting to basic extraction,
What could be verified, not
The possible pull of alloys, not
The wishful benefits of the unseen.

9
Coach said to drink no water
during practice. We'd cramp,
he said, and water guzzlers
were losers who would run
from battle. He'd witnessed
foxhole fear, the piss and moan
of cowardice. There was war
waiting for us in Asia,
and nobody on this team
would do less than good, he'd see
to that, fifteen laps, fast breaks,
a scrimmage, and the night
he switched us into darkness,
lit flares in four corners
of the gym. You keep that ball
moving, he said. You take it
to the hole and crash those boards,
firing his starter's pistol,
advancing while we screened
and rolled, moved without the ball,
more than ready, he said,
to invade any school
who thought "battle-tested"
was just a chalk-talk phrase.

10
After the expanded war stripped
our student deferments, we sold
self-pity in the flea market
of the dispossessed, borrowing
lake front for beer and girls we hoped
to seduce with new-world sorrow.
By summer we'd be refugees,
selected so low by lottery
we'd lug a small part of ourselves
to a bus and listen for rules.
Those girls would finish college or not,
but that day one of them coupled
so close, so much in a clearing,
we thought she'd pull a train of soldiers.
One of us walked our proposal
forward like a diplomat, that girl
so still I thought my friend had killed her.
I heard "all yours," numbers up to six,
my voice assigning my place in line.
Suddenly, each of the other girls smoked.
The sky became a two-way mirror.
As if heaven were behind it, I stared,
repeating what I'd bid on, turning
away, drinking and looking across
the water as if glare were important.
I could see better with my back turned,
remembering dogwood, the burgundy
of that blanket, the fraternity crest
centered under her passive thighs.
I erased dandelions with my shoes.
And when I heard Number One walk away
I didn't flinch, so he could have left
or helped that girl, because when I turned,
finally, the empty space had reformed
among those sweet-scented, flowering trees.

## 11
A week later, a whore in Cleveland
asked me what I wanted for ten dollars,
whether I was scared or queer, hesitant
in Hough, where race riots were months away.
I was playing my last tournament
tennis for a church-related college.
The next morning, I would lose my match
to the one black player in the conference,
and what was I accomplishing
with my doubles partner, the two
of us so white outside the blues bar
we festered like pimples shut up
by stupidity and cowardice.
I said there was nothing she could do
worth ten dollars, said it so measured
and clear to myself that my partner
agreed when I stepped off the curb,
skittering beside me the three blocks
back to where the races mixed, then,
more slowly, two more to where we slept.
"Edison Medicine," I said, quoting
the one person I'd met who'd been sent
to shock treatment. "Look here," he'd murmured,
so softly and so soon after
he'd picked me up, I thought he'd opened
his pants or his set of photographs
would feature nude boys, not Edison's
early film, the electrocution
of an elephant. Didn't I know
the first electric chair was built
at Menlo Park? Didn't I know
they tested dogs and horses and cows
before the first prisoner took minutes
to literally cook? Didn't I see

my body as meat? "You look in the back,"
he said, "and guess," and I swiveled,
saw milk cans, and said nothing at all
while he described the explosions
they'd make if we wrecked or tore through
the wrong Ohio pothole. I was
considering the crimes of elephants
and the ones I'd been lately committing.
"Has you thinking, doesn't it?" he said,
right about that, offering beer
with the early warning of attack,
making me think of opening my door
like a school bus driver each time
we reached a set of railroad tracks.
I didn't ask out. I didn't ask for
the next bottle from the six-pack
between the worn seats, tough enough
to flee Youngstown, Ohio, with
the cargo of possible bombs.
Just before my school, the neighborhood
turned to bones. Forty minutes I'd worked
to ask no questions. In two more,
I knew the pedestrians I'd meet,
the likely rides if I decided
to leave again. Behind barbed wire,
one night shift had parked a lot full.
Pretend you're driving to work, I said
to myself, imagining I could use
the machinery inside those walls,
identical sculptures lurching by
on black, rubber belts, all of us
busy with building the one thing.

12
Now I can buy a video filmed
From a dog's point-of-view, the camera,
Apparently, two feet from the ground,
The subjects those a dog should love:
A duck chase, car rides, a cattle roundup.
"A tape," the brochure claims, "your dog can watch
Over and over," twenty-five minutes
A long time for my dog to watch
Anything unless I train her,
Unless she knows to stay put, flattened
Against the car floor when we cross gravel,
What she hears at the kennel, at the vets.
The way my first son, not quite two,
Screamed when the signal flashed to turn
Left at the apartments because
He knew what that babysitter did
Before his seven-hour shift expired.
Now I can tour the ninety-nine test sites
Of Yucca Flat, hear the anecdotal
Evidence of poisoning dismissed.
Now the theory of hormesis says
Chernobyl will save lives, condition
The Russians like an invisible coach.
And now I'm offering one story
About pathfinding, how I learned
The clues of crossed sticks, the secrets
Of stones arranged into landmarks
In the manual I memorized,
The troop so far ahead nothing
Of them remained but symbols.
Now I'm learning the Roerich sign,
Three dots triangular in
A circle to protect against
Destruction. I'm turning wishful

Among hex signs for caution
Of every degree, something like
The tripled sticks or stones which warn
Comprehensively of danger:
Quicksand, cliff, poison ivy, wasps—
Simplicity's hope, not the demands
Of perpetual poison, something
Cartographers of the toxic need
For the long trip to the future.
Fifty thousand years, durable
As plastic, their signs must signify
The shriek of STOP. Reconvened,
The Voyager Committee tests
Symbols for flying to aliens
At the far end of half-lives.
Consider them children, they're told,
Who find inexplicable etchings;
Consider them Scouts who would flee
The permanent gesture for danger.
Or else they will gather for the slow
Levering of rock, the unscrewing
Of threads, waiting to see what will
Be lifted to the light, what might scream
Through the noise of insects, the shifting
Of dust, the chatter of elements
Emitted from a billion tongues
Like legacy's Esperanto.

## Schmaltz

My mother's old bacon grease filled a jar
That sat among flour and sugar and salt
As if that unlabeled glass held one more
Kitchen staple. 100% fat,
100% thrift—the smoked flavor
Worked its way into eggs so we could eat
More meatless breakfasts. Or no eggs at all,
Just that grease, with green onions, reheated.
That meal took timing, taking the rye bread
To the barely hardened, sopping up *schmaltz*
Like uncles who drank coffee to cut it.
Such richness stayed overnight in the mouth
Where German melted into the English
Of memory, its sentimental schmaltz.
People my age were forgetting the waltz,
The fox-trot, and my father's sad box step.
What would be left, my mother worried, when
Conventional dances were gone? When thrift
Was laughed at? And all those warnings about
Salt and fat, the satisfaction of grease?
Already there were complaints about Heinz,
The soups my uncles made. Pittsburgh was home,
Now, to high blood pressure and heart disease,
All the Germans fleeing to the suburbs
Where bacon was drained, salt never slathered
On the crisped skin of chickens. My mother
Said we could shimmy it off in no time,
Doing the Twist and the Mashed Potato,
The dances of the slim who'd never heard
Of real *schmaltz* and the terrible success
Of learning place, those who wouldn't admit
To grandfathers who ate pure grease and lived,
Who'd punched in for fifty years and carried
The company's gold watch to prove it.

## The Terrors

*A house cleaned will be visited,*
*A house unkempt will live alone.*
My mother, during the week, ended
Her stories in sorrow; my aunt,
On weekends, finished hers with fear:
*The little boy's house got so dirty,*
*The neighbors burned it to the ground.*
Outside were Stalin and the Rosenbergs,
The out-of-work and drunk, and those who
Suffered the great sin of shiftlessness.
*There was a boy who saddened his mother*
*So often she turned into rain.*
*There was a boy who slept so much,*
*His mother buried him alive.*
Outside was school where I'd follow
Directions or else, remember the maps
They had drawn and scaled for my walking.
*A boy, once, had to live in a box*
*Because he forgot his way home from school.*
*A lost boy, at last, grew skinny*
*As straw and blew into a fire.*
In the world of regret and anger,
Each of the women who waited
For me in first grade and day camp,
In Sunday School and the houses
Where music was taught by the half hour,
Had stories about boys who failed.
And so what? If I could read them,
They weren't about me; if every
Student could recite them, they were
No different than news, only public,
What the lettered world notices,
Not the personal, the terrors
We know variously in our hearts.

# The Spiritualists

On television, this evening, stories
Of premature births, an astonishment
Of medical miracles, the problems
Which follow--children crippled, babies
Precarious with pneumonia, deaths
Of the weakest, like the son of a friend
Who showed slides, one night, each of them
Seconds apart in sequence during
The first day of a forty-hour life.
He spoke for himself and his silent wife,
Explained complications and symptoms,
The inevitability of loss.
And the last of those pictures, a head shot,
Stayed through his story of heaven,
How families were reunited,
Keeping me quiet about the woman
Who painted the face of a lost infant
On her breast. Who sat in a cabinet
In the dark and waited for parents
To accept the possibility
Of contact. Who spoke to the departed.
Who bared the beautiful face
Of their dead child and thrust it through
The shadowed, sized opening
Into the dim light for viewing. Who asked
Joyful parents to extend their hands
To brush the soft faces of their children,
Repeating the name of the resurrected,
What I couldn't do, even then,
Staring at the lost, cyanotic child,
Thinking of reassurances,
The roll calls for the briefly living,
What sends us back to simple light.

# Light Enough to Be Lifted

Each evening, after dinner, from April
To October, my neighbor weeds his lawn
By hand. To ensure it's perfect, he says,
Chemical-free, throwing one arm toward
Three treated lawns we face. I keep trim,
He says, by stepping outside before drinks
Or dessert, and he leaves me to sum the pounds
He's never added through the discipline
Of hands in the soil and think of the woman
Who aborted her fetus so she'd be
Light enough to be lifted to heaven
During the Rapture. Of the man who built
A life-sized Jesus from toothpicks, counting
The square, the round, the flat and sandwich kinds
To sixty-five thousand separate sticks.
What weight of needs we carry. What fat so
Difficult to trim we butcher ourselves
With beliefs. I look down where the first thread
Of plantain might show itself, imagine
Seed and spore, the tangle of conception.
Below the earth, in Texas, this country
Has stored thirty-two billion cubic feet
Of helium. Just in case. Starting with
The threat, once, of possible blimp warfare,
Continuing through the astonishing
Catastrophes of the surface which lifts
As if the Rapture for inanimates
Were beginning, all the beautiful things
Soaring toward the heaven for possessions.

*Blood Ties* (2002)

# The Tentative Steps of the Obese

Lately, the news has been following
The man who's been lying in bed,
Too fat to rise, for fifteen years.
Now he's lighter by a hundred pounds,
Standing in his doorway, but he can't
Come out today, says, "I'm not ready,"
Though he may just be exhausted,
Puzzled that anyone would care about
The tentative steps of the obese.

Someone says, "He ate like a sweeper,"
And I title him *Fat Man Hoovering*,
Remember what I've learned about
The invention of the vacuum cleaner,
How the concept came to Cecil Booth,
Who put his lips to carpets and sucked
Dust to the ecstatic proof of choking.

Booth's hotel room had residue
For a million tests, maybe a year's
Worth of feasting for the dust mites
He didn't see, those trenchermen
On his carpet working nonstop
At feeding, growing invisibly fat;
And as the news drives elsewhere,
The dog looks up and listens and goes
To the door to growl at the unheard,
And all I'm believing, suddenly,
Is our personal range of senses
Has shrunk. That we could see those
Dust mites once. That we noticed what
Swarmed and fed. That we nearsighted
Ourselves to forget them, forget what
Towers over us, huge as the newscast's
Fat man, who has five hundred pounds to go.

And I'm following the dog's loud lead.
And I'm thinking, let all of these tenants
Step outside to the eyes of someone.
Let them blink a shy astonishment
At the lenses that admit them. And let
Them be changed and go on changing
And float like dust mites, their bodies
So light in death they rise from our
Carpets like souls, ascending, perhaps,
To ceilings or settling again on our beds,
Gone to some paradise of lost skin that
Tumbles from the nerve ends of the living.

# The Extrapolation Dreams

*Villard de Honnecourt, a French architect, wanted to use the perpetual-motion machine he designed to power "an angel whose finger turns always toward the sun."*

### 1 Brownian Movement

The blizzard was ether.
A few minutes walking
and all the superficial
parts of me were prepped
for surgery. I was
hazy to be home, to leave
my share of the town's
teenagers stuck inside
the weather of stranded,
weekend school. There's
staying awake, I'd thought,
living in the gym with
students; there's pain
horizontal snow won't numb.
And what was a mile
in a Buffalo whiteout?
Fifteen minutes, twenty.
New York wasn't some
Jack London snowbound
deathtrap. I told myself
two thousand steps would
end the cold. I dreamed
counting could put up
panels, that four walls
and a roof could be built
by hundreds, heat to follow.
But that storm witched me
zigzag to two thousand
and nowhere but the blank
deep of the street until
the dark smother of freeze
held its pillow over my legs.

Another thousand, I said,
for sure. And there were
other houses; I didn't need
my wife and children.
After three thousand strides
I could live anywhere
indoors. Surely, I'd reach
a porch that the drifts
hadn't erased. Surely
some family would open
a side door and gather,
astonished, in the hallway,
to see who they'd saved,
who'd returned, prodigal,
from the swine of that storm.

2 *Coriolis Force*

Today, the silver-anniversary reunion book in the mail, autobiographies by my classmates that begin with Lyle A, a surgeon who's living in Harrisburg, who has a green belt and a son in diapers. Then Susan A, whom I don't remember, complains that working full time keeps her from doing anything else. Etcetera, I think, though another book I've been reading explains that each member of my class has spun maybe one step to the side since we've written our stories and mailed them.

Listen, it says, because you live north of the equator, you slip eastward through each moment you move. On your street, it's seven hundred miles an hour that the world is spinning, and, uncorrected, you could slide to your town's river and splash, Icarus of the physics book. I understand. When I walk my mile to school I correct for the quarter inch of slide, allowing for slippage so I don't miss where I'm walking again and again like a child's first day of baseball, a father finding a fat, red, plastic bat, saying, "Here now, try this," and guiding his pitch to where he anticipates the arc, believing he knows the strange physics of children.

Such spinning that flings us sideways. I discover, among my class, a list of our early dead, someone whose wife has died, someone with a daughter killed, and I say goodbye to all of the clipped-from-my-yearbook absent as if they might have moved south, choosing another hemisphere so that they might twist backwards, slide the other way until we might see each other again, a sort of heaven rounding the planet from the opposite side.

3 *Inertia*

Each night the senior's dream of sex and blood,
Waking to the groin buzz at the temples
While high school deflated and I believed
Some thing, for once, might differ. That winter,
On my life's coldest morning, Gus Brickner,
The Human Polar Bear, lowered himself
Into the Monogahela River.
He swam and smiled. He stammered bare-chested
And dripping beside a thermometer
That claimed eighteen below. The weatherman
Shivered and joked until I turned him off
And walked to the school bus stop, hearing snow
Squeak like mice under my Converse All-Stars.
The bus driver motioned me to hurry,
But I kept listening. He waved and honked,
And after I slowed, he hissed the door shut
And drove. Thinking how that school bus might slide
Off the highway and plunge through river ice,
I watched for faces at windows and saw
Nobody, remembered how the Ice Age
Had driven glaciers to right where I was
Standing; how they had receded without
Reaching the spot where, an hour south of me,
Gus Brickner was probably repeating
"Enough"; how you could verify their length

By examining the sides of pits dug
In the earth like the craters for the start
Of missile silos in America
Or Russia. Or Cuba's photographed holes,
Unfilled just before that winter began.

4 *Entropy*

Because my mother has died, because I visit
To comfort my father, who refuses to move
One thing she owned, I see how Christmas stalled at gifts
Opened but unpacked, how her medicine's arranged
By frequency: Crystodigin and Almodet
(Once daily), Cytomel (three times per day), duties
I know, with the weak heart. Percocet (as needed,
For severe pain, no refills), and I wonder at
The gap between the heart's demands. Then Nitrostat
(As needed, for chest pain), those pills the films' foolish
Grope toward as they tumble one room from relief,
This urgency of labels leveled to a kind
Of democracy, a haze of help from which nothing
Can emerge. Although I've learned my own medicine
From the tablets I take, twice daily; the capsules
I swallow, as needed; and the vapor I breathe
In the lapsed-lung darkness, lying back like Proust, whose
Life I've learned for my job, whose asthma bedded him
For years. He didn't take Theolair, Optimine,
Ventolin; insisted, finally, a huge black
Woman was chasing him. So she caught him. So now
My father strains to speak, tries, "Well, did you sleep good?"
To unmuzzle the morning, and I answer him,
"Good enough," as if truth might trigger prescriptions,
As if accidentally we might talk, as needed,
Swallowing to save our faulty selves, carefully
Speaking from the confluence of our altered blood.

## 5 Brouwer's Theorem

This snow is nothing
but an hour's cover.
Where I walk, the grass
returns, and these prints
that don't refill point
nowhere dangerous
unless I should last
a thousand miles north,
as far as I've been:
Beaupre, St. Anne's shrine
stacked up with crutches.
I trudged by braces
while it snowed in May.
I took color slides
and considered each
premonition pain
in my doubter's limbs,
how nothing there could
repair any part
of me, so far north
that week I retraced
the minus steps, ones
that lead right up to
the vanishing point,
something else we learn,
paying attention
to the snow lecture,
perspective lesson.

## 6 Perpetual Motion

Once upon a time, in the public schools,
There were Sputnik children, closed in classrooms
Until someone learned to launch satellites
That would orbit forever. We were trapped

Between science and math, waiting, waiting
For Rumplestiltskin to spin our homework
Into gold. He never arrived, of course,
But this winter my Chicken Little son
Is saying he fears the fall of space junk,
That the Russians could kill him as he sleeps
Dreaming himself into old age photos.
Tithonus, I think, one more fairy tale,
Although I tell him we're safe, ignorant
And lying as if I expect Villard's angel
To turn, to keep turning, to swivel
Its way toward eternity like myth.

How ludicrous the theories, and how we
Hypothesize again, guessing Bobby,
Billy, Jack, and Dave as if we were rich
With chances, as if machinery were
As simple as common names. That promise
Wheel was whirled by hammers, surrogates for
Water, and Villard moved nothing at all.
There were rockets on the television news
That tumbled and exploded and locked us
Tighter to physics and calculus, and
Now I'm starting one more wheel, expecting
A miracle even though the demon
Of foolishness has caught me by the shirt
To show me how easily things are jammed:
The dream of building. The dream of these words
We use, believing they sound like something
That goes on as perfectly as singing
In your head the records you love, sounding
Exactly like Ivory Joe Hunter,
Like Jessie Belvin, like Johnny Ace, names
From another kind of children's story.

I have blueprints on my desk; I'm writing
To scale and I'm failing to form all sides
At once as if the blind spots of migraine
Pinwheel through my translation. And I think
There is failure in this paper and ink,
The letters level as always, precise
As store displays, nothing for sale or use
Though we believe them voices, time lines drawn
From page to page to page like hammer wheels,
Satellites, the extrapolation dreams.

## The Donora Geomancy

*In 1948, nineteen people died in Donora, Pennsylvania, during a weekend of heavy smog.*

By reading the scattered patterns of seeds or sand,
By inspecting leaves or twigs, by tossing small things
In numbers and guessing, we might foresee
The first day of suffocation, the coughing
Furious throughout the thick, postwar inversion.

No one, then, read seriously a splash of stones.
No one murmured and looked up, terrified to moans
By the crossed and parallel handful. No one
Sang the prophecy of bone, Donora's deaths
At the end of the history of ruined lungs.

Now we regather the ashes to carry them
Like icons, renege the lead of the waste future.
Now we pursue the smogged, discredited past,
The quiet struggle of zinc workers who perform
The gasp chorus before smother interrupts.

Donora locked in power's smoke-filled room, hidden
In closets and under beds; Donora pulling
The sick to adrenalin's miracle,
Pushing the old to the great divining
Of flowers scattered over a drop of coffins.

On the hillsides, the last, late cabbages in soot;
On the hillsides, sheep gone black where anyone
Could carry remnants from the wire works
In his fist, shake them loose upon the ground
Which bears no grass, and begin to study.

Five days of pollution's narrowed throat. Five days
In the dry mist which rehearses the wheeze and pause
On the four-step staircase, the afternoons
Of the darkness funerals where mourners
Pay attention to the coughed prayers of neighbors.

And not prayer, but rain which scoured back shadows
Into the day. Not prayer, but the zinc works shutdown.
And so short a closure, so short the rain, so few
Moved away in the following months, the world
Returned to its own assurances:

Belief in beads, belief in tumbled ash and bone,
Faith of the hundreds who recovered, the thousands
Who suffered unrecorded, who worked again,
Comforted by how the near-dead revived, how grief
Is not compulsory in the age of science.

# The Great Chain of Being

> *Three generations of imbeciles are enough.*
> —Oliver Wendell Homes, 1927

## 1 *Too Little Air*

There, on her carpet, we sat
Our year-old sons, and my cousin
Watched me count the handicaps
In her first-born until I froze
Like four legs in the headlights.
An accident, the doctor had
Told her, too little air, citing
The brief thesaurus of cause.
I nodded like someone saving
His job in an office of lies.
Her son crawled like he'd lighted
On the huge, invisible web
Of God. "My sister's boy has
A problem, too," she murmured.
"Both of us are moving closer
To cities so this never
Happens again." Too little air
In Pennsylvania, in Georgia.
Too little air in the room
Where we stared from one boy to
The other, so quiet, so long,
We might have been practicing
Conservation, as if that room
Had been sealed by landslide, and
We were finding the essential,
Slow rhythms of survival.

## 2 *Vulcan and the Fire King*

Planet Vulcan had to be there, hidden between
Mercury and the sun. What else, according to
Newton, could vary an orbit? What better name
For a planet so close to molten, in theory,
A hideout where Satan might be perfecting hell?
But when Vulcan stayed unspotted, the mystique of
Congruence stuck science to the keyhole until,
Soon enough, the impetus of impatience brought
The first sighting, the second, astronomers claiming
Discovery. There, they said, pointing the lens. There.

And there, the nineteenth century, fireproof women
And men headed playbills by surviving tortures,
Taking advantage of expectation's effect
On the eyes, one way we tend the infrastructure
Of error, relying, like Christians, upon
The necessity of the unobserved, as awed
As the audience for Chabert the Fire King, who
Climbed into his personal wood stove with raw steaks
And emerged, later, with a meal, well-done, sitting
To eat after visiting Vulcan's test kitchen.

Soon enough, a royal family of magicians
Could enter fire, reappear unscathed, diluting
The Bible with the commonplace of illusion.
Soon enough, the frequent tracts on explanation,
Scientists clamoring their revisionist clues
Until, finally, the appearance of the cage
Of fire, this wood stove open in front to appease
The jaded. There, they said, there he is, believing
Again, the Fire King standing in towering flames
Like the personification of a planet.

3 *The Little Moron*

In health class, eighth grade, we learned
The descending categories
Of the Stanford-Binet.
You couldn't do worse, if you
Made a mark, than idiot.
We knew one who loved lime soda
And laughed at the end of a leash
In his back yard. We saw imbeciles
Bused in and out of half-days
In the resource room, and we told,
In the halls, little moron jokes:

*The little moron was playing
With matches and burned the house down.
"Your daddy's going to kill you
When he gets home," his mother said,
But the little moron laughed and laughed
Because he knew his daddy
Was asleep on the couch.*

We laughed and laughed at everything
The little moron did. Why would
He take his ruler to bed? we asked.
*He wanted to see how long he slept;*
And he wanted, joke by joke,
To bring the dead metaphors
To life—time, butter, and fire
Flying out his busy window.

"That will do," our teachers said.
"Three generations of imbeciles
Are enough," the Chief Justice said,
In 1927, supporting
The Eugenics Record Office,

Which wanted to sterilize everyone
Deemed unfit. Harry Laughlin,
Superintendent, hoped to eliminate,
In two generations, the submerged tenth
Of our population. He meant the blind,
The deaf, the orphans and the homeless;
He meant the poor and the stupid,
And the Supreme Court backed him up,
Finding a "clear and present danger"
In the family tree of the Bucks—
Who were illegitimate and poor;
Who were Emma, Carrie, and Vivian
Who made enough of these morons,
Declared deficient at seven months
After this expert testimony:
"There is a look about the baby
That is not quite normal, but
What it is I can't quite tell."

None of the Bucks, it turned out,
Was a moron like the one who took
His ladder to church for High Mass,
But Carrie's sister was sterilized,
Too, for good measure, and here is
The rest of the little moron's story:
He climbed and sat on top
Of his stepladder. He looked down
On the congregation, who were all
Looking down together. And looking
Down from the stepladder of research,
I can repeat the rosary
Of heredity, say *Fragile X,*
The syndrome which chains my cousins,
Their three imbecile boys, one

Generation enough, in this case,
For a chromosome passed down
Like a family job. That I'm
My mother's exception, in theory;
That my sister, who carries,
In theory, has no children.
That Vivian Buck managed
The honor roll in grade school
The year before she died. That chance
Blows the finest glass from this
Illusionist furnace, my gifted sons
Taking, like their father, those
Skip-a-grade intelligence tests.

4 *The Verisimilitude of Purpose*

Angels descend with lightning. The great fire
Of autumn signifies the bright palm prints
Of God. In Syria, five hundred years
After Christ, the infinite gradations
Of God's love were found in the natural
Light of all things by Dionysius
The Areopagite. The harmony
Of dusk and dawn. The iridescence of
The chosen. Even the angels absorbed
More or less of God's light, according to
Their nature, and they formed a chain of choirs
Graded toward glory. Who would believe in
The clumps and clusters of chance? And who would
Dare witness for the flaws of the learned?

In the Great Chain of Being, angels move
Above us, brutes below. Edward Tyson,
Comparative anatomist, believed
He verified the church's sleight-of-hand.

He studied a chimpanzee, expecting
The link which hooked to man's. One thing it liked,
Happily, was wearing clothes, a good sign
For the brute next door. And the first night out
At the bar, it drank itself to all fours,
Then altogether down, comfortable
With vice. Drinking is fine, Tyson explained,
But this damned knuckle-walking has to stop
Before you can model for the Great Chain
Encyclopedia: Practice . . . practice . . .
Tyson needed that chimp to walk upright,
Something snug between the large apes and us
For the arpeggio of the Great Chain.
But in one of Tyson's old plates, the chimp
Uses a walking stick; in another,
It ambles away, holding a rope stretched
Overhead like a commuter's hand rail.
And as for the pants? In hours, they reeked, were
Changed, then stunk again, refusing to chord.
Those chimps were exotic as Africans,
Who were one step above them, several steps
Below the British in the writings of
Charles White, biologist, who needed,
A century later, the alcohol
Of theory to enter the fire of doubt.
The Great Chain of the Upright, he bellowed,
The eighteenth century ended, the jaws
And foreheads of the apes translating as
"Africans." The American Savage
Was next, the Oriental its neighbor.
And White worked his way, by facial features,
To Europe, and, by extrapolation,
To the Greek ideal in antiquity.
Here was an apparition of theories,

The verisimilitude of purpose.
Praise orangutans, he published, because
They submit to bloodletting. Praise them twice
Because they take the African as slave.
Damn the sweat (not enough) and smell (too much)
Which binds Africans to the brutes. And as
For intelligence? In the golden age
Of assigned place, the white man bound to God,
Form followed function. Once, when I had to
Recite the heroic couplets of Pope,
Passages chosen from "Essay on Man,"
The Great Chain of Being jangled and clanked
Until the bored superior beings
"Show'd a Newton as we show an ape,"
Another thin theory taken to heart,
Immanuel Kant, in the Charles White years,
Looking to Jupiter, the planet of
Sufficient size to support God's higher
Beings, links between us and the angels.

*5 The Gifted Test*

The year I was asked to skip a grade,
The tester asked for the quick recall
Of body parts, current events, and
Trivia. For science, I mentioned
Ptolemy, the sun as God's spotlight;
I sequenced Copernicus, the church,
And Galileo. He smiled and read
Me puzzles like the one about Bill
Meeting his mother-in-law's only
Daughter's husband's son. What relation,
He questioned, is this person to Bill?
His son, I blurted, not bothering
With the proffered pencil, and I thought

He'd be astonished because I could
Calculate, in seconds, the equal
Number of quarters, dimes, and nickels
To get nine dollars and sixty cents.
I knew how many 9s I had to pass
Counting from 1 to 100,
And how to slosh water back and forth
From five quarts to three to finish
With exactly four. I thought the expert
Loved my top-scale score, would show me off
To every teacher in the district,
But my parents voted *no* and *no*
Before he spoke. That winter I built,
After a snowstorm, a model of
The solar system according to
Johann Kepler. In our yard, I rolled
And shaped a huge ball for Jupiter
And a white, scale-modeled mound of sun.
I sized the planets to match, measured
Circumference and the distance from sphere
To sphere. I needed the neighbor's yard
For Pluto, and when the frost planets
Seemed plain, I gave them their moons to scale,
Snow berries and packed pebbles of ice.
At the end of the street I snowballed
Another star. I stood a hundred
Million miles from it, thought of my house,
And readied myself for ignition
Because surely, in all that snow, some
Life had formed and evolved to greet me.

*6 House Wrens*

My cousin was telling me about progress, care, and love. Her husband was tossing a ball to our ten-year-olds, casually and carefully by turns. A step closer, a step back, handicapping the distance. My son, later, listed all of the unlucky signs of coordination and speech, the long face and big, floppy ears of the donkey. And later still, this year, my son in college, hers on clean-up crew, and two other cursed boys from her sister, heredity taking three branches where the gypsy moth of chance laid its eggs, we bunch at our reunion where that trio flaps frantic with motion. One of them knows the name of every bird at the feeder by the pavilion. I'm told to say, "What's that?" each time one settles, and he shouts, "House wren," waves his hands, bites them, screams, "House wren" for the next and the next, laughs and laughs at my ignorance. And whether it's the same bird, three different ones from the same species, or he's bluffing like a parrot, I ask again, looking to where my own sons are throwing horseshoes for the first time, already bored with *ringer, leaner,* the simple language of play.

*7 Stitches*

Turning into teens, we bunched in those last
Vacant lots beside the tracks where no one

Would build. Beneath our feet, the cackling of
Eggshell glass, the rasp of cinders, static

Through the retelling of improbable
Erotic stories, the tentative beer

And Camels keeping us perched on the lines
Scratched in the dirt where Holt and Bradley fought,

One of them snapping enough right hands to
The face to etch humiliation.

Bradley crawled. He bleated until a tail
Grew behind him, until his lips disappeared

And all we saw were teeth just before he sprang
Snarling with a brick, opening forty

Stitches worth of gouge through Holt's crew-cut scalp.
And that exam-nervous night, none of us

Knew what we recollected while Holt told
His parents about plunging from a tree.

And then we wished for wounds, the thin sweat tracks
On our chests turning scarlet the next time

We practiced the tumbling agony of
The stunt man down each return-home hillside,

Hearing the highway diesels drive by tough
As armies, clutching ourselves when we rose

Where prefab houses were exploding from
Shell craters, and there, in variations

We could not see, our features would crawl up
Inside us like shy, unwanted birthmarks.

8 *What the Lecturer Showed Us*

Some mornings the chimpanzees skip breakfast,
Hike as one to where the Aspilia grows.
They gibber reluctance, chatter complaints
Of bitter and vile, but all of them gulp
Its leaves, clean a branch like children frightened
By the household god of famine-to-come.

The purgatives of the rain forest, home
Remedy for parasites, for fungi—
And we may smile, following them on film
Carried here by science—but now, we learn,
The oil of the Aspilia destroys
The malignant cells of certain tumors.

Thus, we're instructed by the pharmacy
Of the primates, watch the sick chimp who drags
Herself to the foul bush of Vernonia
To chew its leaves, swallow the juice. We cheer
Her next day recovery, how she grooms
Herself again and forages for food.

And, of course, in the natural selection
Of medicinal plants, the ignorant
And stupid will swallow poisonous leaves,
End their faulty genes with an incorrect
Prescription. Pay attention, survivors
Lecture, to pattern, color, texture, scent.

Eat these stems during the rainy season.
Take two of these petals for climate change.
And here are the aids for fertility,
Their counterparts for prevention. And there
Are the howling monkeys who can diet
For daughters or sons, who eat acidic

Or alkaline to shift conception odds
For the $x$ or the $y$ of sperm. Watch those
Howlers who feel betrayed, perhaps, or trapped.
They grind the leaves for induced abortion,
Take care of themselves without consulting
Doctors, lawyers, politicians, or priests.

## 9 *The Polygamy of Doubt*

In the polygamy of doubt, we see the overhead wires
Of the rope trick, the man who threads it upward.
Some snake charmers, cautious, sew shut their cobras' mouths
And perform hourly, racing starvation and the next
Careful stitching. And certainly, though Tyson's chimp
Never got drunk again, some animals lack discipline,
The elephants who go back to beer, chug twenty at a time
To forget, some theorize, the end of the open range.

Someone else claims the dinosaurs forgot everything
But the drugs of flowering plants in the centuries
They first flourished. Those lizards gorged and got high;
They overdosed and died in an apocalypse of the giants.
We've laughed and laughed at their idiot ways, more
Foolishness in the great chain of brutes who rattle
The links of their life spans -- the sestina of dog years,
The sonnet of the hamster, the haiku of the may fly.

And we believe so much in the epic of our lives,
The photographs, the slides, and the long pauses
For our stories which enlarge the past until our memories
Are edited to accept the anthropic principle, how
Everything has led to us, the fingernail filings,
In one image, of the king's long arm of time,
Entering one more theory as if we were the magicians
Who amaze by slipping *into* impossible restraints.

10 X

My uncle keeps a chart of ancestors,
My mother's great, great grandfather series,
Their occupations parenthetical
Beneath their life-spanned names. Tailor, tailor,
Tailor, it says, fading like an echo
Through the nineteenth century and stopping,
1782, in Germany,
Five generations fixed in one village
Before the coming to America.

The great chain of a construct. All but one
Of them died from lung disease; I use
An inhaler for cats, pine trees, the dust
From these redundant flow charts, checking for
Myself in my mother, my sons in me,
Until the white linen of reunion
Settles us, and my cousins, the mothers
Of imbeciles, watch their husbands cut ham,
Butter corn, prevent their sons from choking.

When Einstein accounted for the shifts in
Mercury's orbit, the Vulcan sightings
Ceased. Someone works, now, to identify
The monkey gene. And on a million hats,
This year, the X of a dead man who worked
To break one version of the static chain
Of being. And in some illustrations,
The X of the early cross worshipped by
All my cousins who take their sons to church.

On documents throughout the world, the X
Of the marks made by the illiterate,
Repeated and repeated, mimicking
The signature. And in the protective
Mimicry of nature, the viceroy looks,
Now, to most birds, like the monarch, the one
Butterfly they've learned not to eat because
It gorges, as a caterpillar, on
Poisonous plants. And even its name is

Mimicry, one more step in the art of
Disappearance we practice, vanishing
From the sight of angels who swoop down to
Comfort us. They see the near six billion
So similar we might all be noxious
Gathered here at the X which marks the spot
Where we've driven to celebrate births and
Anniversaries. And finally, we
Assemble in one huge, rented room to

Face the camera of each parent. The light
Is weak and varied near the north window.
The children are sullen or self-conscious
Or bored with the afternoon's past. "Ok,"
I say, "ok," finding the three imbeciles
Who are gripped on the shoulders, two-handed,
By grandmother, mother, and carrier
Sister, each of those wild boys smiling
And still, momentarily, for my flash.

## The REM Sleep of Birds

For years, no one was watching, when, in sleep,
The stories some suffered by night spun long
With plots that vanished. The REM-sleep novels
Erased themselves, turned to the wolf-child tales
Of the difference-wishful. Though there's good cause,
We've learned lately, to find yourself early
In those nightmares (the sooner, the smarter).
It's good to have narrative, metaphor,
Because the overdressed dream is a sign
Of the adult lurching from the mists of
Nursing and crying, awake in the crib
With no language to use on the woman
Who arrives to hover, float overhead
In her own feathered fear. Listen—now we
Know the rapid eye movement sleep of birds
Is more than flutter, that imagery slides
Through the ruffled darkness among the leaves
Where swallows dream of falling; starlings dream
Electrocution on the power line;
And sparrows dream of a world of windows,
Glass labyrinths, the insistence of flight.

## Why We Care about Quarks

Because something deflected the fired electrons.
Because emptiness, suddenly, seemed crowded, and
The invisible, three bits of it, needed a name
After *aces* was rejected, that opener called
Before a fourth dot could fill the proton's hand.

Because some things can't be named by committee,
Approved, like *ampere,* like *moron,* by a show of hands.
Because one physicist had read *Finnegan's Wake*
And remembered "Three quarks for Muster Mark,"
German for cottage cheese or forced-rhyme Joycese.

Because an invisible zoo can be named by whim.
Because each quark could be christened like a pet:
*Up,* then *down,* then *strange.* Because *charm* was found.
Because *beauty,* the fifth, appeared on the doorstep,
And theoretical *truth* belongs above it.

Because there may be more, anything possible
Where the eye can't enter. Because symmetry
Builds models, and the octagon's fresh flavors
Will need to be named: *paradise,* for instance.
*Eternity.* As if the inferred, invisible

Structure were proof enough for the alleluias
Of hope. Because someone believes in the force
Of color, the power of purple or infrared
To bind as many as eighteen quarks, building
A tower or ladder or beanstalk which will

Surely lift us to the sky-blue ceiling, our children
Gathering to steady us from below as we feel
For the trapdoor seams, rap and listen for the hollow
Sound of entry, reciting immortality names
Like delirious disciples of ascension.

## Forecasting the Dragon

When Huang Ti, the emperor, sent Hsi and Ho,
The imperial astronomers, to explore;
When they shipped out for every place east of China,
The lands of Fu Sang, to see if the heavens changed;
They sailed to America, west coast, arrived so
Long ago their voyage seems historical hoax.

When they tired of Guatemala, of Mexico,
Four thousand years before Commander Columbus;
When they made it back to China, they reported
To their boss, who listened and nodded and returned
Them to their science, to forecasting the dragon,
The one who crossed behind the sky to eat the sun.

When the solemn gongs still worked. When a multitude
Of clamor could retract eternal night if throngs
Gathered soon enough to drum fear in the serpent
And the sun's first missing mouthful were broadcast, what
Hsi and Ho were hired to know, dating the dragon,
Predicting its hunger for holy Huang Ti.

And when Hsi and Ho failed, the oriental sun
Bitten by surprise, the beaters not alerted.
When, bored by the familiar Chinese sky, they were
Drunk and delinquent, the silly world saved, this time,
By the delicate appetite of the dragon,
The two were executed by their lucky lord.

Or so one history says, although here, in others,
Are the Hindu missionaries in the New World,
Six hundred B.C., and Brendan, the Irish priest,
Five-fifty A.D., and then all of those Norsemen
Who came and went, sighting after native sighting
Of the strange-skinned seamen, the oddly-featured gods.

So many disembarkings of swords and armor,
Bibles and beards. So many indecipherable
Creatures, they turned as common as the green and blue,
The huge heads and slender bodies from the saucers
I read about on Sunday mornings, stopping, once,
At the true-life adventure of Joe Simonson,

To whom spacemen had given a pancake. I stared
At his photograph. He had the flapjack as proof,
Holding it up to the lens, and I was eating
Cereal, the breakfast of aliens, raising
My bowl as if posture and a double portion
Could transform my body into a rainbowed hulk.

Mary King, in England, had met Master Jesus,
Who had flown here from placid Venus to hand her
The Twelve Blessings of extraterrestrial love.
Her son, she claimed, was sacred, and anyone can
Guess the counterclaims, the scoffing, the tabloids' joy
Until the Mercurians flamed down in Belgium.

But when my neighbor, just now, tells me about lights
Where they could not be; when she describes colors in
The night woods, babble turned to language by her skin,
I say nothing of Pancake Joe, Jesus in space;
Nothing of Balboa, Magellan, how oceans
And continents were titled by selective claims,

Diaries turned to scriptures.  These ships touch and flee
As if Earth's surface were shore. In each galaxy
Are Vespucci Papers from a thousand planets,
True histories of expeditions, the wonder
Of contact, the loss of faith, how the universe
Has been labeled, bit by bit, in a million tongues.

## The Hunza Dream

> *The Hunza, from northwest Kashmir, are the only group of people known to be free of cancer.*

1

After this coal town lost its jobs,
After anthracite packed and fled,
The entrepreneurs arrived, wrote
*Hydroponics* on their government grant
For gardeners and glass, low-interest
Revitalization loans. Now hundreds
Of greenhouses lie on the leveled slag,
Tomatoes going green to pink, half
A million madly swelling out of water
Inside this paradise for vandals.

2

The last coal has wound its way eastward,
Lost itself to barge and train. A mile
From the greenhouses, a culm-bank rises
Higher than any hill in the county,
Sits sparse of growth like the cancer-scalp
Come home from treatment for the hot spots
In the body when they flare like mine fire,
Rumors of bankruptcy, default on loans.
And this evening I watched those houses
From my steel-blue car, parked by myself
Like a lure for entrapment waiting for
Lights, the lonely, or the Quasimodo
Look of the law. And when the darkness clung
To the stalks, when none of those choices
Came, I backed, turned, and crept to the highway
As if I'd thrown a body from my trunk.

3

How we rock-a-bye our children
Through inevitable day-mares,
My daughter blood-tested last week
And winning her lottery with
The mono ticket, seven days
Asleep instead of clinic drives.
Surely, she must understand that
Cells default, a boy she's danced with
Dying tonight a year after
Sitting for that needle. She's heard
His odds, at least, quoted, because
He hadn't mishandled canning,
Plutonium, or sex. She's seen
Eulogy write itself despite
Diet, safeguards, desire's control.
And after the doctors removed
His bone marrow, after they cleaned
And changed it to something he might
Live with, they put it back, and he
Brightened, then bloomed, then turned to husk.

4

Always, in the collective wish, there are parents
Reading the stories of the laying on of hands.
In this house, in those rooms, in that office their lips
Are moving to the rhythm of the faith-spun words
As if reading like children might ease the entrance
Of the Hunza dream. In the gospel of remissions
Is the prophecy of promises. In the gospel of cures
Is the hearsay miracle of the absent apostle.

## Calculating Pi

> *Pi has been calculated to 480 million decimal points.*
> *—Newsweek*

Printed out, this means six hundred miles of digits,
A paper carpet from Pittsburgh to Chicago
For high tech absurdists who might be tallying
The sheep they've imagined before sleep, the fat flock
They've columned and counted like the cartoon restless.

Who might be lapsing into the dreams the awake
Have: numbering loss, summing the hours, repeating
The simplest algorithms for despair. Who might
Be fool-proofing the warhead, eliminating
Error, so deep in the silos the soldiers know

Their computers are exact, whether they're sending
The missiles to Moscow or its suburbs. Pi checks
For typos, dust specks, and cosmic rays. Pi's perfect.
Pi's a sitter's lullaby. Hush, it sings, don't cry,
Crooning soft verse to soft verse to infinity.

# The Universal Language of Waiting

My grandmother waited for her husband in German,
For the coming of Christ in Latin. Her neighbors sang
Or screamed in Slovak and Polish, Croatian and Czech,
Believing so much in the rhythms of love they banked
Their hearts like the furnaces in the long-struck mills.

Some of those women swept me close with their brooms to growl
The ground rules of sidewalks in gutturals that promised
To use one end or the other on my thoughtless face,
Their dogs snarling the same sentences of woe until
The street turned into the squalling radio of fear.

Some people suddenly speak a language not their own.
Some people start to write what they recall in spellings
That bond in the quick Spanish of the first Mexican
Family on Prospect Street listening to speech so strange
They thought everybody in Etna emigrated
From a village bound by the rope of related tongues.

A director, once, made a film in Esperanto,
Transforming dialogue to mystery, believing
Each exchange became as eerie as the incubus
Who stole the souls of sleeping women while he slathered
Each scene with subtitles or dubbed over flapping mouths.

That film waits for Esperanto's rise, the world joined hands
Around the campfire of common language. My grandmother
Told me, in English, about the eighty-pound ice heart
Omaha carved to lure Sonja Henie back to town,
How it's shrunk to sixty pounds, still warehoused, speaking to

The dead in the universal language of waiting.
Like Ludwig Zamenhof, who believed he could form peace
With the Yugoslavia of good intentions;
Like all those diplomats who listen on headphones
To simultaneous translations, each of their nods
Staggered by the varying degrees of rephrasing.

## The Air of Delicate Pastry

Francis Battalia, years ago, ate stones
By the spoonful, chased them with beer and shook
The sack of his stomach for evidence.

Soon, stone eaters flourished. The thinnest drank
Water to flush their gravel, fueled one cult
Of reduced calories, early converts

To the slow furnace of zoologists
Who extend, these days, the lives of test mice
By diminishing their charted dinners.

In our country of sad diets, we choose
The stones of low sugar, low sodium,
The rocks of low fat and cholesterol.

We suck and roll them back our tongues to gulp
Doses for the fears which keep us cautious.
Which bite brings the AIDS of the arteries

Or the stiff botulism of the heart?
Though he made them, my father wouldn't eat
The fat lady-locks and thick whoopie pies,

Refusing their sweet, white sculptures of creme.
Lard and sugar, he told me. A little
Water. Fool's food, he said, like the corn starch

Of bargain pies, the refined sweeteners
Of icing he tasted, judged, and spit out
While he slathered it for millworkers,

Baking from midnight till morning, stopping
With doughnuts turning gold in the deep-fat
Fryer. He ate wheat bread, the rich custard

Of eclairs. He explained fiber and eggs
And the legitimate sugars of fruit.
And he praised the natural holes in bread,

None of them like the homogenized air
Of Wonder loaves, their dough a miracle
Of emulsifiers, whipped and balanced

Like flavored scoops of soft ice cream, perfect
Squares of processed cheese. And then he described
The air of delicate pastry, how it

Lightens the richness of butter, how he
Folded and sheeted, folded and sheeted
Until that sweet dough spread so fine and light

It released the breeze of desire, the breath
Of gratitude, what works to support us,
The air from which we never grow estranged.

## Class A, Salem, The Rookie League

We were drinking for free, bumming beers
From the past-their-prime by claiming
Ourselves Pittsburgh prospects, fire-ballers
Who'd broken in, last summer, in Salem.
We'd gotten a look in Columbus,
Three innings each in a courtesy game.
"Candelaria," we said, taking
Refills. "What a party he threw
When the Pirates called him up that night."

We settled for Iron City, draft mugs.
It was semester break, sophomore year.
In three weeks, pitchers like us were due
In Bradenton, Florida, to prove
Ourselves for Double or Triple A,
And we wouldn't come back to this bar
At Easter unless the two of us
Were released, disabled, or home
For a sudden death in the family.

We said my mother was sick, my friend
Had a tender arm. We said we'd leave
Tickets for this tavern if either
Of us made Three Rivers, and drank four nights,
Underage, with men who supported us
Like fathers. They wanted names, who

To expect from Salem in three years,
The vets we'd met on their falls to sandlots,
Factories, or bars like Emerico's,
Where they'd name, in turn, Al Oliver,
Dock Ellis, or the Steve Blass Syndrome,
Cite the strange, sad case of his lost control.

We were twenty miles from our old school,
Two districts from any fans we knew,
But there, one midnight, sat Mrs. Cook,
Giving us her speech-class, critical look.
She could have offered *slower, louder,
Breath control.* She could have recited
A roll call of our gradebook names, summoned
Us to the front of a fist-filled room
With the forensic demand for truth.

Glazed-green, the bar's surface suggested
Sea stories where the careless drown
In a tangle of cramps. We carried
A beer to her booth like homework;
One of the men who loved baseball
Slid in beside her. "From the Pirates,"
We said, trying to enunciate
Like athletes, setting our last story
Deep as we could in the farm system.

## The Local Cemetery

I went by myself, late
In the summer, looking
At first, over my shoulder
Like some clumsy spy.
I walked to the brightest
Cut flowers and paid
Attention to last week's date,
The name of a woman
From my street. Her husband
Had come here yesterday.
He had looked, I supposed,
At his dates, 1914-199_,
Giving himself four years,
And I have been with my father
When he stood on the grass
And said, "You can always
Find me here." He gestured
And meant me to think
Of the nearby plot as mine;
I kept walking and found
Whole families, like ours,
Together for a hundred years,
Settled in from Europe
And never moving again,
Never thinking of moving,
And even now, my sister
Has moved back to Pittsburgh,
Two miles from my father,
And asks when I'm coming home,

Says she has purchased space
In the Garden of Dreams,
Which, so far, leaves me out,
Kicking the earth hundreds
Of miles away, picking up
The one stone I've seen in all
Of this grass and sailing it
Into the trees where it rattles
And falls into silence.

# Enlisting

Every list came to school:
milk, dimes, savings bonds.
On the teacher's desk
sat the bathroom list
and the fountain list.
They'd squeal on you.
They'd tell Miss Hartung
you were smoking or carving
filth upon a wall.
There was a list in the air
that beat up sissies,
that circled Harold Martin
and signed him up
for a second tour
while the list for teams
chased us across a field,
yelled from the bleachers,
stood by the sidelines
in a gang. We shrunk
inside our uniforms,
hit and curled by tackles,
air nowhere near our lungs.
Not then. And not while
those lists were posted,
the ones that flew us
to Asia, the third
of seven continents
on a list we copied
from Harold Martin,
who stopped reporting us
after he read our list
all over his unprotected,
third-world body.

*Writing Letters for the Blind* (2003)

## Dragging the Forest

After the First Aid Meet, after our patrol
Revived Mike Hofaker, who played the victim,
My father, the Scoutmaster, settled us down
With our scores for bringing back the heart and lungs.
Correctly, we'd stopped bleeding, and perfectly,
We'd treated shock. We'd made splints from newspapers
And neckerchiefs, eased them around our problem's
Broken bones and carried Mike Hofaker through
The hall by makeshift stretcher to prove safety
For the judge who'd scored us second, total time.

"You think you could save someone?" my father asked,
Driving me home along the Allegheny.
I looked at the water, but my father said,
"Up there," nodding toward the steep hill of forest
Where, he started telling me, he'd spread his arms
And walked in a line one hundred Boy Scouts wide.
"We were flanked by men," he said, "who repeated
'Fingers touching.' The boy had been lost two days.
We hiked up, moved sideways, walked down. We sidestepped
And started up again before three boys screamed."

"The lost boy, of course, was dead," my father said.
"He was tied naked to a tree, eleven
Copies of the out-of-date *Sun Telegraphs*
Folded up inside his bag like an address."
I thought my father meant me to be careful.
From where we were driving the river was black,
The woods thin enough to take the sun's last light.
Scores came on the radio. The teams were Pitt,
Army, Syracuse, Notre Dame. From bottom
To top, the width of the woods went to shadow.

# The Busy Darkness

*What the Optometrist Said*

The eyes facing forward means predator,
Along the sides of the head declares prey.
Better here? Worse? Any difference at all?
To find our way in darkness, we must have
Six times more light than panthers. To make out
Danger, we need ten times more light than toads.
Try these. They'll fit a face as thin as yours.

The rhinoceros sees so terribly
It charges large rocks, occasional trees.
You can stop squinting now. It's a habit
You've formed through neglect. Don't you see yourself?
What do you think? Your eyes aren't corrected?
That there's too little light? That you can't see
What's approaching before it gets too close?

*Writing Letters for the Blind*

For fifteen cents, or twenty, in the script
I'd mastered from Miss Sperling, I wrote
Saturday letters for Bill Nelson, who
Sat blind with a white cane beside his chair.
He loved the letters in return, the lines
Scratched out in pencil or blue ball-point ink.
This is Gary writing, he had me say,
And women, often, when they wrote, added
Postscripts that began *for your eyes only*
As if I wouldn't read their words aloud.
*Such a dear*, they repeated. *God bless you.*
*We should all have such a generous son.*
When one woman had her daughter write me,
She folded that page inside her letter
So Bill Nelson, holding the envelope,

Smiled and said, "It's a good one, two pages."
Straight out, that girl said her mother wanted
Us to meet, that the slope of my letters
And my way of crossing *t's* showed I was
A boy to be trusted when we were grown.

Before he paid me in nickels and dimes
From a change purse open on the table,
Bill Nelson measured every coin by touch.
A test, for sure, because everybody
Knew the blind heard better than the sighted,
And I passed for months, not stealing, until
A woman mailed a dollar post-scripted
For me. So quietly, it lay upon
The table that I read, "The five dollars
Are for Gary," giving myself a raise.
Would Bill Nelson believe I was worth it?
Would he consider his coins and add them
Higher in my hand? In fact, I hoped so,
Because I wouldn't steal, taking nothing
From the blind but what I thought I deserved.

*The Era of the Vari-Vue*

"He can see shadows," my father told me,
"Bright light and pitch dark," as if Bill Nelson
Had time-traveled from the Bible's first day.
From a front seat, squinting, I could copy
My teacher's chalked words; from my desk, I could
Recognize friends' faces four rows away.
The spring I was failing that blackboard test
And the exam of the curveball, I thought
Everybody saw with the soft focus
Of myopia, hunched down to pages.

In the first, fad years of the Vari-Vue,
My father brought home plastic-ribbed pictures
Of Plymouth Landing and Christ on the Cross.
The proper distance, he said, the right tilt
Of the head until I wig-wagged Pilgrims
Ashore; the eyes of Jesus to heaven;
And signed, bobbing my head, a small, slightly
Blurred, Declaration of Independence.

Dog-at-the-hydrant. Cow-over-the-moon.
Finally, I wore glasses. By the time
I mastered contact lenses, I could shift
Nixon's eyes in the White House windows, could
Surface my children's skulls and nod my wife
To bones, flicking her forward, fast or slow,
Like mutoscope women you could undress,
Once, for a nickel. Now, for quarters, men
Can lock up in booths to watch looped films, choose
Sound-suffused channels on the porn network,
Sighed syllables of acquiescence flung
Like dots on this page I'm holding tonight,
In the gallery of unimportance,
Trusting they will leap up as holograms.

I'm staring at a near-wash of purple,
Coaxing "halved spheres" or "peeled fruit" off paper.
I'm deciphering instructions, learning
The sure ways to 3-D without glasses,
Pulling the page haze-close, one simple step
To "deep sight," the *trompe l'oeil* of computers
If we posture ourselves like the near-blind.

You enter the page, the inventor claims,
And I imagine the third dimension
Of pornography, toxins surfacing
in lakes, futures embossed by tainted blood.
I call each of my chattering, clear-lensed
Children to these pictures, say "hold this close
And stare," prodding them to levitate balls
And fruit, say "pear" and "globe" as if these were
Rorschach blots for the willingness to see.

*Remedies*

The Sioux believed in opening the eyes
To the dust of bezoar stones they found
In the bodies of buffalo and deer.

The British, once, believed in the power
Of baking a black cat's head to powder
For blowing in the eyes three times a day.

And some of the nearsighted, more squeamish,
Have worn gold earrings, trusting the bright loops
To recall the radiance of vision.

*Pushing the Black Thread*

> *Hagop Sandaldjian, the world's only microminiature sculptor, was described as "a very calm man."*

Last night I couldn't thread a needle.
I took it under three kinds of light;
I licked that thread; I ran it between
My fingers and thought luck, finally,
Would pull it through while I remembered
The man who sculpted between heartbeats,

How he kept his hand steady enough
To carve Snow White and the Seven Dwarves,
Red Riding Hood, and Cinderella,
Each sculpture so tiny he placed them
In the slim eyes of sewing needles.

What he carved can't be seen unaided.
For all I knew, his lost Mickey Mouse
Deflected my thread that threatened art.
"May all your dreams come true," that sculptor
Etched along one hair, but he used lint
For Presidents, dust motes for the Pope,
And I pressed my chest, at last, against
A high-backed chair, studied my pulse for
The instant of greatest calm, pushing
The black thread, failing, pushing again,
Listening and listening with light.

*Not the Worst*

Not the worst, the doctor says, matching
Me to his patient list. Not the worst,
Sounding so rehearsed I imagine
The patient who only sees shadows,
Welcoming, whore-like, whatever moves.

In the country of perfect vision,
Would anyone record what was seen?
And gone into exile, would those eyes
Wear themselves dry with excessive use?

Look. Gaze. Watch. Stare. When every edge turns
To haze, when persistent fog compares
Our hope to the hell of indistinct,
We listen for the breath of beauty,
The custodian of clarity,
Sweeping, unable to keep us clean.

*Better, Better, Worse, Better*

Last night I woke and saw nothing and knew
It was my Bill Nelson dream, the one where
He makes change in the dark, handling each coin
In his black purse until he's satisfied
Which ones are proper. I imagine him
Cheating himself; I imagine keeping
His quarters and lying about the blind,
How they mistake coins the way I misread,
With my fractioned vision, the brief rebus
Of road signs, the puzzle of passersby.

This evening, I trust my sight to the eyes
Of my neighbor, the optometrist, who
Listens as I say, "*Our Hearts Keep Singing,*"
Describing the album by the Braillettes,
Three blind women beaming good attitude
And bright hope from their cover photograph.
"It's on *Heart Warming Records,*" I finish,
Taking air puffs between blinks to confirm
It's not glaucoma that's sucking my sight.

I stammer, "Better, better, worse, better."
I hear diopters, thickness, the great curve
Of this year's inadequate correction.
The doctor hums the ceiling tunes. Follow
The light, he croons. Now ignore it. Although
I want to say "How?", half-expecting him
To switch it off, smiling in the darkness
At optometrist humor. "Worry you?"
He'd say. "Got you to thinking?" plummeting
The room to black, waiting for my answers,
My optimistic eyes still dilating,
Whether or not I'll be sadly clever
With compensatory, heartfelt singing.

*How the Optometrist Encouraged Calm*

During panic, when your mouth dries,
Breathe out until the count of six.
Breathe in until four. Count slowly.
One, two, three . . . more slowly than that.

Try to remember it's just your brain
Mimicking the symptoms you dread:
Breathlessness. Dizziness. The chest
Going tight, tingling through the hands.

Better yet, recognize your fear
Is only anticipation.
Fight it with facts. Be specific.
Darkness is danger not yet here.

# The Fathers I Could See from My Room

The father who lifted sample cases from his car,
The father who carried a briefcase full of grief,
The father who tallied the pros and cons of spending—
What did they do in those offices where nothing
Was built, no customers to please? What changed
By their leaving early, by their sickness, retirement,
Or death? We had moved to where one father mowed
His lawn in white shirt and tie; we'd left behind
The street of fathers who entered factories
And mills at seven or three or eleven.
I knew what they did because they detailed it drunk
On weekends when the world could wait for the things
It wanted. When Sputnik circled the planet,
When the Communists made something we couldn't buy,
We watched, on the news, the melancholy arc
Of America's latest failed rocket. The fathers
Who wore suits kept doing the work that makes nothing,
And one of them, while I slept over with his son,
Brought betrayal home at midnight, what we shouldn't hear
About faithlessness. Below us, in the driveway,
His Lincoln looked like it spent all day in an office,
Like a woman had starched and ironed it. That father
Let his wife talk herself into leaving. My friend
Propped himself so long on his elbows I wanted
Something like mumbles to squeeze under the door,
Sounds so simple they could turn into regret.

## What Color Did

*When disease strikes, it is because the colors of the body's elements have fallen out of balance.*
    —Dinshash Ghadiali, inventor of the Spectro-Chrome

Color mattered. My father held out shirts
And ties like a ring-bearer and waited
For my mother to match. And while she was
Deciding, he offered her socks and pants,
The two sport coats he owned in brown and blue.
In the early days of the pastel shirt
For men, my father seemed too old for choice,
The simple era of the white shirt gone,
This time for good, so much depending on
Color, it was almost medicinal,
Curing shyness, uncertainty and fear.

Not the first time for that. *Normalating,*
As Dinshash put it, was what color did—
In other words, therapy for the sick.
See, he advertised, the elements most
Common in us are linked to hues: The red
Of hydrogen, the blue of oxygen,
Carbon's stoplight yellow, nitrogen's green.
See, he explained, shining filtered light bulbs
On the skin above his patient's organs,
Here is the way to brighten or dim them,
Regulating the rainbow in ourselves.

Color mattered. My father faltered when
Patterns came to his shirts, pinstripes and plaids,
Madras and paisley and fields of flowers
That made a perfect match impossible.
Close enough, my mother would say, holding
Those shirts and ties to the natural light.
Close enough, yet my father turned tight-lipped
In public from her doubt, unbalanced through
Sundays until he pulled on the full green
Of his uniform for work, sweeping up
After children who wore clothes like models.

Not the first time for that. Dependable—
What the boss called him as he aligned desks,
Arranged chalk by color while my mother,
At last, purchased "The Healing Scarf," praising
Its silk and its rainbows dyed to contain
Every shade needed for recovery.
She studied its guide to color's power.
She learned the locations for pain. She wore
The scarf on her skull to balance her brain's
Intricate rainbow, and trusted the shade
Of X-rays, the felt color of chemo.

Then my mother died, her rainbow of clothes
Packed and donated. My father recalled
Three combinations, washing and ironing
The plain shirts--blue, beige, and gray--laying them
Out with the ties and socks on my sister's
Unused bed, repeating them fourteen times
Through a year of Sundays and twice during
The six Wednesdays of Lent, rotating through
Good Friday and Christmas and Thanksgiving,
Funerals and weddings, as many as
Twenty times a year then, the simple shades
What he knew of color, dressing himself
Three ways for God, one for work, until he
Became all silence, unbalanced, and dark.

## Marking the Body

My doctor, a woman, knows how shyness
Shrinks men gone vulnerable in the groin.
She waits while they unbutton or unzip,
Turns from me this morning, giving me time
To excuse myself with a just-learned story:

Behind a curtain, once, women would mark
A female doll exactly where they hurt:
Just below the breasts, for instance, covered
By the doll's uplifted arm, they charcoaled
A cross; low in the belly they scratched an X.

My doctor knows that history. She says
My male doll has X's over the lungs,
Cross-hatches on the throat, skipping the spot
For this morning's mark, the way I've never
Been this slow to undress for her instruments.

My doctor, who knows when eternity
Begins to form far out in the future's
Ocean, covers her hands in the latex
Of discretion, reaches for me, and says,
"The feet of those draperied women were bound."

My doctor, who would have passed that Barbie
To the discreet hands of a physician,
Examines me like a familiar doll.
She breathes high on my naked thighs, that air
The first that fails to stir the stiffening-blood.

She pivots, strips her gloves, and I follow
The intimate lines of her breasts and hips
To the softness of myself, fixed until
She turns, finally, in the last moment
When we both are deciding what's arriving.

# The Early History of the Submarine

In the handed-down writings of Pliny.
In Herodotus; in Aristotle.
In DaVinci, who fears The Flood's return
And sketches his own elaborate plans.
In failures. In the men who construct them
And drown. In Cornelis Drebbel, who sinks
And resurfaces, confident as God.
In his passengers. In King James the First,
Who demands a ride. In closing that hatch.
In sliding under the surface, the king
Watching the hull, listening to those walls
For the limits of greased leather and wood.
In Drebbel saying five, ten, fifteen feet.
In their settling and the king exhaling.
In the oars they pull together. In talk,
Finally, of windows and speed and air.
In Drebbel, at last, slowing his breathing
To give the king a larger share. In joy.
In surfacing with wishes he's prepared.

## Otherwise Healthy

Twice this week, choosing from near the bottom
Of the list of phrases I rarely use,
I've murmured "otherwise healthy" as if
It explained the history of allergies.
The foot doctor who lives nearby has died
From a bee sting despite his antidote.
The five in my family, slouched on the deck
From summer dinner, shake our heads, listen
To my daughter tell us, a second time,
She swallowed liqueur speckled with gold dust,
And her throat shut tight as if it wanted
Nothing more. Though after she gasped and wheezed,
After her friends begged the bar for doctors,
She saw strangers stand to say "what?" and "how?"
Like magician's children, the evening's whim
Deciding, then, to soundlessly inhale.
"I could have died a metaphor," she says,
"The woman with an allergy to gold,"
And we list the odd possibilities
Of "sunshine" and "moonlight," "the songs we love,"
How we turned up our favorite music
As we walked outside on this clear day, just
Before sunset, daring the light and dark.

# The Plagues in Order

For Children's Day, for the church pageant
Performed by the primary classes
Taught by the Misses Shuker and Swope,
We were the plagues in order, changing
Costumes while Moses spoke, returning
Ten times to taunt the unbelievers.

In crimson sheathes, we were the river
Turned blood. Masked and hopping, we were frogs.
And when we heard, crawling and flapping
As lice and flies, the *ohhh* of adults
From the pews of Etna's Lutheran Church,
We knew a day's praise was seething for
The holy revenge of our costumes.

Like cattle, then, we went to all fours,
Lowing and listening to Miss Swope,
Who spoke for God from the balcony,
Promising the plagues to everyone
Who hardened his heart like a Pharaoh.
Like Egyptian cattle, we buckled
And fell to the side-sprawl of dying.

Look, there was more. We all wore white hoods
Circled by the red of boils, flung
Brown rice as hail before we chattered
Like locusts and swarmed off to black-sheet
Our bodies, waiting for Miss Shuker
To switch the church to darkness we made
Darker, shivering like just-freed souls.

And when we caught the collective hush,
The first-born among us dropped and died,
The rest solemn despite being blessed
By the lottery of birth, standing
To the sides like two halves of a sea,
Walking in wide pairs from front to back
To the street as if we expected
Our chastened families to follow.

## Birds-of-Paradise

After surgeries, after one knee
And then the other were scraped and cleaned
And made comfortable like the dying,

I swung myself on crutches, then limped,
Then slow-walked near normally until
This next breakdown of cartilage and bone.

Tonight, my father says, "Now you know,"
Phrasing satisfaction or despair
With his old rhythms for speed and bluntness.

Together, we slide and shuffle down
His stairs, do the awful one-step
To the music of irreparable.

For all it matters, for comedy,
I call out my turning radius
In a short expletive of self-pity,

Watch my father manage the minute
He needs to rise from a chair and lurch
To his collection of canes by the door.

"Some mornings," he says, "I wake thinking
My legs are amputated, yet there;
That I've been revised like your best poems,

My knees small hinges that bend just air,"
And I believe, in that moment's rhyme,
That he's prepared for me by rehearsing,

That before mobility's rapture,
We'll redesign ourselves by omission,
Taking away all the common parts

By which we are compared, becoming
Birds-of-paradise, which, because the legs
From the first specimens sent to Europe

Were removed for easier shipping,
Were thought to perpetually fly
And live by eating the dew from heaven.

# The Magpie Evening: A Prayer

*When magpies die, each of the living swoops down
and pecks, one by one, in an accepted order.*

He coaxed my car to start, the boy who's killed himself.
He twisted a cable, performed CPR on
The carburetor while my three children shivered
Through the unanswerable questions about stalled.
He chose shotgun, full in the face, so no one stepped
Into the cold, blowing on his hands, to fix him.
Let him rest now, the minister says. Let this be,
Repeating himself to four brothers, five sisters,
All of them my neighbors until they grew and left.
Let us pray. Let us manage what we need to say.
Let this house with its three hand-made additions be
Large enough for the one day of necessity.
Let evening empty each room to ceremony
Chosen by the remaining nine. Let the awful,
Forecasted weather hold off in East Ohio
Until each of them, oldest to youngest, has passed.
Let their thirty-seven children scatter into
The squabbling of the everyday, and let them break
This creeping chain of cars into the fanning out
Toward anger and selfishness and the need to eat
At any of the thousand tables they will pass.
Let them wait. Let them correctly choose the right turn
Or the left, this entrance ramp, that exit, the last
Confusing fork before the familiar driveway
Three hundred miles and more from these bleak thunderheads.
Let them regather into the chairs exactly
Matched to their numbers, blessing the bountiful or
The meager with voices that soar toward renewal.
Let them have mercy on themselves. Let my children,
Grown now, be repairing my faults with forgiveness.

*Standing Around the Heart* (2005)

## Standing Around the Heart

We stood, in health class, around the cow's heart
Miss Hutchings unwrapped on her desk. Inside
And out, she said, we need to know ourselves,
Halving that heart to show us auricles,
Ventricles, valves, the wall well-built or else.
Her fingers found where arteries begin.
She pressed the ends of veins. Richard Turner,
Whose father's heart had halted, examined
His hands. Anne Cole, whose father had revived
To cut hair at the mall, stepped back, turning
From the entry to the steer's aorta,
The four chambers we were required to know.
While we watched, Miss Hutchings unwrapped the hearts
Of chickens and turkeys, the hearts of swine
And sheep, arranged them by size on the thick,
Brown sack, leaving a space, we knew, for ours.
We took our pulses. We listened by way
Of her stethoscopes, to each other, boy
To boy, girl to girl, because of the chance
We'd touch. Those butcher hearts warmed while I dreamed
Of pressing my ear to the rhythmic heart
Of Stephanie Romig, whose breasts, so far,
Had brushed me one time while dancing. And then
Miss Hutchings recited the quart total
Of our blood, the distance it must travel,
Leaving and returning, all of the names
For the necessary routes it followed,
Ending with capillaries so close
To the surface, we could nearly reach them
With our lips and tongues, rushing the blood to
Each of the sensitive sources for joy.

# The Eternal Language of the Hands

The surgeon Celsus, at the time of Christ,
Said the right hand should operate
On the left eye, the left hand should invade
The right. He meant the interns to practice
From the weak side like switch hitters,
An old strategy which makes us smile,
But the smug health of the moment
Turns a page in the book of longing:
I looked left, then right, at the pictures
My father showed me—the husband, the wife,
Through five generations that ended
In German scrawled unintelligibly
Across the back. I was young enough
To believe, because he had lived
With grandparents who spoke privately
In German, he would translate the three pairs
Born somewhere other than Pittsburgh.
I expected a second language to
Enter me like the left-handed layup
I practiced each day, but he said German
Was forbidden like taking the Lord's name
In vain, that he'd shaken off Kraut and Hun
And Heine, slurs I'd never hear because
We'd changed. He might as well have tried,
Like some, swallowing a child's raw heart
For beauty and love. Consider
How many cataracts Celsus removed,
Inserting his needles, nudging them
Off-center like wind-blown grit. Left, then
Right-handed, thousands of years before
The surgeries we wait for. My father,
The baker, rolled sandwich buns with both hands
At once, circles so tight you couldn't tell
Which had been formed from the left or right.
Like Celsus removing clouds and teaching
Those miracles to disciples
In the eternal language of the hands.

## The Buchinger Limbs

In the year I wrote small, everything
I knew could be copied on a page
If I practiced until I mastered
The perfect penmanship to succeed.
A corner for school, thin lines along
The bottom where lust and pleasure spoke.
Inch of family, a column of friends,
The short sentences of school and work.
I was a tenth-grade wonder, shrinking
Myself to stumps of ink, but my aunt
Told me tales of Matthew Buchinger,
The man with flippers for arms and legs
Who wrote seven Psalms and The Lord's Prayer
As the curls of his self-portrait hair,
Reducing those articles of faith
To miracles of calligraphy.
So tiny, she said, each of those words.
Think of holding the pen with a fin,
Using that grip for the common sense
Of achievement. On the news, reports
Of thalidomide. In Germany,
Where her father had come from, cases
Of the newborn with Buchinger limbs.
Look, she told me, so many deformed
We will soon not notice the dreadful.
If you can learn anything at all,
The smallest words will drive you blind.

## The Uses of Rain

We sat, in geography, for nine weeks
With water, a marking period of rain.
We followed the dittoed diagrams
Of water's efficient recycling—
Precipitation, evaporation,
All the clouds we memorized for exams:
Cirrus, cumulus, the great thunderheads
Like the ones Mr. Sanderson called us
To watch at the windows. Snow, he told us,
Was nature's cheap ice cream, more air in drifts
Than water. A barometer, he said,
Could thrive inside an injured knee. Then he
Made us read the names for irrigation,
How crop rotation and the geometry
Of plowing could safety-net the earth.
He taught the proper times for lawn sprinklers,
The folly of building in the flood plain,
And we remembered the time tables
For tides, the value of delta, wetlands,
And the extraordinary ecosystem
Of the ocean. And though we conserved
For extra credit, though we catalogued
Our care, we took our test, turned it in,
And listened, books closed, to Mr. Sanderson
Tell us the story of the crested bustard,
Whose desire is triggered by the sound of rain.
"Because it lives in the desert," he explained,
"Its courtship dance must be timed just right."
He held our stack of tests to his chest
And walked among our rows. "In zoos," he said,
"In captivity, those birds begin to dance
When they hear a keeper's hose. They prance
To the simple sound of cleaning, believing
That rain will water the luck of their children."

## Sweet Things

All the way through doughnuts, I sang along
With the radio because they were the last
Sweet things I laid my hands on before my shift
Was over. My father was busy with icing,
Blending color with different degrees of sugar,
And then he had an hour of pastries to fill
With custard and fruit to compete with the rolls
On television which cakewalked to the oven.
In the bakery, time raised bread and browned it.
Time hand-rolled sandwich buns, carried pies
And coffee cakes to cool on countertops,
None of them strutting off their pans after
I stepped into snow, inhaling with the joy
I thought I'd earned before dawn, driving
The station wagon four miles to where
My mother was drinking sugared coffee
And eating zwieback she'd brought home stale
The night before. I heard news, weather,
And the drive-time deejay play Bobby Vee,
Connie Francis, or some sound-alike
For success because it was time for
The reasonable world to test itself.
And I left that car on the plowed street
So I could say the hell with shoveling
Our driveway with the snow still falling,
Exhaling with my mother before she closed
The door on the Chevy still warm and steered
It back to the bakery in the changing light
To sell to men finishing one shift
Or starting another at the mill,
Each carrying a bag of sweet things
Into the ordinary ends of morning.

## Bringing Back the Bones

I read about the men who maim themselves,
Who amputate fingers and toes and arms:
The man who practiced on pork shoulders and
Put, finally, the shotgun to his leg;
The man who crushed his leg, set it afire;
The multiple cases of men who lay
Their legs across the railroad tracks and wait
As if the world has insufficient loss.
I remember two friends who lost both legs
In cars, others who gave up toes and feet
To diabetes. I want to write them
Whole, bringing back the bones, though my father,
Each time I visit, reminds me my words
Are no different than bread he baked, the cakes
He iced by hand, squeezing out the sweet script
Of birthday names. He shows me, this trip,
The school bus full of old books and papers,
Tells me he's driving them to Aspinwall
For dollars by the ton. We stand, later,
In the leveled lot of the razed bakery.
He scuffs one mark for the workbench, one more
For the mixer, nods at my shoes and waits
Where the dough would rise while I toe the earth
And tell him my tale of the wooden legs
On the child mummy unwrapped in Egypt,
The carbon-dating which said those legs were
Centuries younger than her bones, someone
Opening the grave and fitting those legs,
Someone forming sized feet from reeds and mud.

## Anniversary

We learn, today, a girl who attended
Our wedding has been murdered. Thirty years,
We say, guessing her age—eleven? twelve?—
From the old photographs that help us tell.

We read the articles from three papers—
Cord-strangled, the saw taken to her limbs—
One picture, then another, something like
A legend beginning, something like hell.

Just home with her fiancé, our daughter
Looks at our young selves. The summer evening
Reaches into our kitchen; she helps us
Name the naturally dead, chanting a spell

For her mother's white gown, what my daughter
Will wear, this gift she tries on, beginning
To enter her story, raising the sleeves
To her face, drawing them closer to smell.

# The Weaknesses of the Mouth

There were punishments for the weaknesses
Of the mouth. Two uncles had killed themselves
With salt and fatty meat; an aunt had slaughtered
Herself with sugar. "Each of them knew,"
My mother said, but I was growing
Into the bone-stunting of tobacco
And candy's pimples, "God's way," according
To my mother, who warned me about
The pack of pink gum I found and chewed,
That there were dope dealers who seeded
Desire with good fortune, waiting for
The next day of need, that gum, alone,
Enough to empty my mouth of teeth.
I stopped talking, then, about the warm dance
Of tongue and lips, the moistures driven
By the heart. The first beer I swallowed
Poured warm from three bottles I found
In the half-razed house where old rubbers
Told me there were willing girls nearby.
I had such weakness, I finished the fourth
Long-opened bottle, stepped, minutes later,
Through the lost heat register's empty hole
And stuck at my shoulders instead of
Tumbling to cellar's glass and nails.
It was the last polio summer,
Seven years until my first cold beer,
Reversing the Pharaoh dream, famine first,
Refusal urging my mouth to open.

# The History of Silk

In seventh grade, when we were alone for
An afternoon, no chance of being caught,
Silk was what we sought in our sisters' rooms.
It was enough to hold silk and name girls
Who might be shedding the slick things we touched:
Pajamas, panties, lace-trimmed slips with straps
Designed to be nudged by passionate hands.
Three or four together in those bedrooms,
We turned alike, drawing silk things over
Our skin like fingertips, lifting our shirts,
Opening our pants in dark unisons
Of desire that made us refold those things
Exactly, replacing them in order
Until the afternoon one of us slid
That silk over his head to bring himself
Closer to pleasure, and he did, though none
Of us would touch or talk to him, the words
For his body disappeared long before
We knew the history of silk, the way
Taming turned the silkworms from tan to white.
The way, defenseless, but unharmed, they stopped
Trying to escape. The way, become moths,
They didn't fly, how they mated and died,
Without once opening their damp, pale wings.

## Headcheese, Liverwurst, a List of Loaves

Our refrigerator
Opened to liverwurst,
Headcheese, a list of loaves:
Luncheon and Luxury;
Olive, Old-Fashioned, and
The great alliteration
Of Peppered and Pimento.
We eat, my father said,
One hundred million cans
A year, justifying
Our Spam. Three per second,
He figured, and we sat
For sandwiches he cooked
Because I refused them cold.
"You just don't know what's good,"
he said, and I agreed,
refusing altogether
Potted Meat Food Product,
Looking it up, lately,
To find "tripe, suet, beef hearts,"
Memorize the mystery
Of "partially defatted
Beef fatty tissue," to tell
My father, who's laid out
Cold cuts of celebration
For his restored heart, shaking
His head at snouts and stomachs,
All the meat byproducts
I can recall while we spread
Mustard or mayonnaise,

Add pickles and onions
To the short stack of squares
And circles between thick rye
With seeds. And I listen
To my father repeat
"This is eating" before
Our first bites, smiling while
We swallow extenders
And gelatins, relish
The joy of fat and spice.

## Coughing Through the Brambles

Some days the asthma wakes me early,
Makes me walk through the underwater dark
And trust my footing to prescriptions
While I find the shallow end of wheezing.
So quiet, this illness, so unlike
The bark of the common cold, the great whoops
Of the cough more serious that killed
One classmate the winter the whooping crane
Stood extinct, almost, on the front page
Of our Weekly Readers. We watched slides
Of condors and grizzlies and pale fish
We were supposed to care for, and even now
I watch for Harvey Westlake, the sun
An hour away, because his spirit
Might choose to retrace itself, search for
An arrangement of houses and yards
And debris which calls up our childhood,
The dwarf shape of fear whose messages
Stay simple as those folded inside mittens.
For asthma, once, you swallowed spider webs;
For whooping cough, some parents would push
Their children through blackberry brambles,
Those stems which arced to thrust themselves
Back into the ground like living hoops,
Listening to the terrible thrusts
Of air through the constricted hoops of throats.
It was like the laying on of hands
For tumors and tuberculosis;
It was the faith and prayer of my parents
Who passed me through the brambles of eternal
Damnation, expecting answers the way
Some men listen for responses to
Radio waves they transmit to outer space.

The year Harvey Westlake died, I read
A story about the first broadcasts
Reflecting off the edge of the universe
And returning for rebroadcasting.
"O Holy Night," the radios played,
By Professor Fessenden, 1906,
And then Bible verses from St. Luke,
Stutters of stations working toward
The cacophony of perpetual
Retransmission of a billion broadcasts.
And I might pass all of the past's coughing
Through the brambles which run the border
Of the lot I live on, three times each,
One thrust exactly like the others
In distance and direction until
The heavenly white magic takes hold.
And I might lay my healer's hands
On the vulnerable spots of those
I love, trusting the medicinal
Power of faith, but I've weaned myself
From the vanity of prayer, believing
Enough voices are rocketing toward
The imagined edge of the universe,
So many supplications seeking
The thin, improbable antenna,
The unlikely decoding, and then,
So far to return, so many requests,
The everlasting shower of granted
Wishes soaking the astonished
Descendants of the faithful and
The faithless, flooding both with bitterness
And joy, and drowning the need to believe.

# Miss Hartung Teaches Us the Importance of Fruit

The banana is a herb, she said, but
The Koran claims it's the forbidden fruit.
The orange is a berry. Grapefruit is new.
On Fridays, when we opened our lunches,
She lectured on our apples, plums, and grapes.

A President, she said, after hogging
Cherries, died; a French king, over anxious,
Bit the prickly skin of a pineapple
And shredded his greedy lips. Remember,
She said, tomatoes and olives are fruit;

Eat your salads and think of them as sweet.
She brought papayas, mangoes, kiwi, figs;
She taught the origin of the lemon
And the domestication of the lime.
She said there are 5000 kinds of pears,

Doctors who prescribe them like booster shots.
Pick them early, she warned us, or they go
Gritty; let them ripen in your kitchens
Or the cells inside them will turn to stone.
Listen, children, she said in June, the peach

Preserves the body. The Spanish brought them,
And even the Indians learned to love that fruit.
And why not, don't all of us know the way
To everlasting life? Don't we all have
An instinct for the perfect gift from God.

## Johnny Weismuller Learns the Tarzan Yell

For public appearances, for the crowds
Who expected perfection, he managed,
Take after take, to mimic the sound
The studio had built for an ape-child.
Practice was like swimming all those laps
In the pool, building his breath again
To fill the audio needs of Tarzan:
Camel's bleat, hyena howl played backwards—
He couldn't admit to plucked violin,
A soprano's high C added, one
After the other, to his own best roar,
His champion's howl so much a common cry
The audience wouldn't think "explorer caught
In quicksand," "hunter surrounded by spears,"
Not Tarzan loud in the natural world
Where the hybrid voice develops into
The great arpeggio of beast and man.

# The History of SAC

*1952*

In the hospital, in the enormous ward,
Twenty-four iron lungs were breathing for
The tri-state's victims. Nurses paused to murmur
Near each disembodied head, the room
A theater of whispers, the film obscure.
My aunt, their supervisor, held my hand.
I breathed in and out through my sterile mask
And thought of steam irons at the dry cleaners,
My father's two suits tagged and returned
Like pigeons. The smell of trichloroethylene,
How it dizzied, how it followed us
For a half block of store fronts. On runways,
At that moment, thousands of bombers
Were idling in case Truman or Stalin
Decided to end the world. In the sky,
To our north, a shift of squadrons hung
Like the mobile over the face of the boy
In the row to my right, second lung.

*1972*

We drove to a runway's end, the great
Passenger planes lifting six minutes apart,
Banking and turning toward selected cities
Like missiles. We parked and faced the squat cliff
Like the disembarked; the sky became
A belly so heavy it had to fall.
That evening, you clutched yourself by the stove,
The front, right burner coiled red under
A sauce pan poised for boiling. Wait a while,
You said, let's see, and turned the water to LOW.
After the coils went dark, you said

"Yes, again" and disappeared to dress.
The plates and silverware lay bare three days.
A nurse walked the aisles among the isolettes,
So many babies breathing so easily,
I listened for the heavy approach
O apprehension, the water in the pan
Transformed to air, the kitchen turned metallic,
The stove sitting ready as a SAC bomber,
Idling on LOW until you handed me
Our son and dialed it slowly down to OFF.

*1992*

In the AIDS unit, we walk with my sister,
Who has a grant, hundreds of thousands
Of dollars, to study the attitudes
In care for these lethal patients, the poor,
Twenty to a side. I keep to the center,
Curse myself like I do when I refuse
The sturdy rails at overlooks, dilettante
Of the blood. I think of yours in that instant
Which fixes us to eternity,
That son old enough to contract disease
From his ward approach to sex, and when we
Reboard at America's newest airport,
Enough runways to handle the SACs
Of a hundred nations, my childless sister
Says, "We're going global," sweeping her hand
As if she means to peel off the horizon.

## In Films, the Army Ants Are Always Intelligent

Water and fire again, we think, watching
Natives dig a trench, lug the gasoline
To its banks. It's the white man's solution,
Some land owner protecting investments,
All those years of cheap labor just lately
Paying off. Ants, after all, are ants, but
Understandably, he's a bit nervous
When his workers chant, fumble with magic
In a pouch. Savages, he's learned, always
Sense when the absentee gods should be called.

And we might wonder, while the cameras pan
The rain forest for troops, if these things rest,
If there's a day along the Amazon
When you could sleep off hard work or a drunk
In safety. And why there's still a jungle;
And why these ants, a million years of them,
Haven't eaten every square inch of green.
There's never a natural predator;
There's only the good sense of travel north
So climate can negotiate with them.

All we're taught, at last, are the miles of them,
That their sign language ripples front to back,
Reaching the billionth soldier correctly.
Remember that schoolroom game, the one where
Miss Harshman whispered a message into
Janey's ear? She turned and whispered those words
To Billy who whispered to Sally and
Thirty seats later you recited them
To laughter that blossomed from the first row?

Think of yourself as sluggard in the rear.
For days, you've had nothing to eat, the ground
You're covering stripped clean ten thousand ranks
Before you. Well, somebody has to starve,
You might conclude, improvisational
In the tropics. But then you feel the word,
Sense *plantation, panic, picnic for all*.
There are sacrifices ahead, some proof
For those parables, you see, when your turn
Finally comes: The early waves were burnt;
The first leaf rafts were sunk; and you're certain,
Dancing before battle, that the water
And fire are gone, that the natives have fled
Or been shot in the back by the owner.
So he's on his own now, self-destructive,
Or maybe he has dynamite, something
Apocalyptic. On the other side
Of the moat, there is feasting. All you have
To do is cross, stepping from one body
To another, to cultivated land.

*The Fire Landscape* (2008)

## The Anomaly Museum

My mother believed in the prophecy
Of metaphors, ignoring the omens
Of our literal street where husbands worked
And their wives kept house. The anomalous,
She insisted, foretold the promises
Of the body, citing the child just born
With fur, the woman with a forehead horn,
And most telling, the boy whose head ballooned
To show us salvation's fortunate sign.

"To make room," she said. "To accommodate
His beautiful, enormous soul," meaning
For me to consider my thoughts, turning
My headaches into hope and fear, making
Wonder from misery so rare, the way
A reader might take these syllabic lines
As one more expression of "look at me,"
Each word a disguise for deformity
Like the airbrushed nudes in the night museum
Of magazines I toured during high school.

Then, while my mother's heart turned commonplace
With disease, I entered classrooms to face
The exhibits for terrible fortune:
The boy with Thalidomide stumps, the boy
Bent breathless by tumor, the girl whose lungs
Thickened to failure. Kevin and Rob. Greer.
I can recollect their names thirty years
Or more since I passed their symbolic selves
In the hall of occasional horror.

All along, my cousins were carrying
Their latent, faulty genes toward the three sons
Who would show that flaw in their sluggish brains,

Those boys calling up the face of that child
Who disappeared inside the great swelling
Of rare luck, the impossible size meant
To console us who need only foresee
The common routes to death, the stroke, this week,
That froze one side of a friend, his voice gone
To the slurred vowels of my cousins' boys.

The truth is that yesterday my friend still
Inhabited such a possible face
I looked everywhere he wasn't. And now,
In the museum I visit by myself,
I examine the bleak pornography
Of anomaly, attentive to how
The plates of one childish skull expanded
Until they burst open like a flower,
So impossible there is not one thing
To do but think of the boy as blossom,
Disregarding the ordinary parts
Of him until they go unremembered
As the busy shapes of nearby tourists.

# Black Veils

I learned the verse where God demanded hats,
Found the reference to veils. For hundreds
Of Sundays, the women around me were
Covered by the lace-like, black strands of tulle.

I saw that men can show their face to God,
Learned that faith surrounds the heart like cotton.
Without it, I would hear my pulse, go mad.
The dead were delivered at once or damned.

The veils were raised by hymns; they fell for prayer,
Fluttered through the long words of the pastor
As if something frail and invisible
Was beating its wings against the fine threads.

The dark veils were as serious as smoke.
They whispered the soft language of the dead—
Mrs. Sowers, Miss Shupe—I knew the names
Like the books of the Bible, Genesis

To Revelation. When I tried one on,
I sensed the dim humility of hope.
When I examined myself in mirrors,
The clothes I wore needed to be undone.

# The Sorrows

Whatever the Sunday, the sorrows kept the women
    in the kitchen,
My cousins and their mothers, my grandmother, her sister,
    all of them
Foraging through the nerves for pain. They sighed and rustled
    and one would
Name her sorrows to cue sympathy's murmurs, the first
    offerings
Of possible cures: three eggs for chills and fever,
    the benefits
Of mint and pepper, boneset, sage, and crocus tea.
    Nothing they
Needed came over-the-counter or through prescriptions
    not bearing
A promise from God, who blessed the home remedies
    handed down
From the lost villages of Germany for the aunt
    with dizzy spells,
For the uncle with the steady pain of private swelling;
    for passed blood,
For discharge and the sweet streak from the shoulder.
    In the pantry,
Among pickled beets and stewed tomatoes—the dark,
    honeyed liquids;

The vinegar and molasses sipped from tablespoons
        for sorrows
So regular they spoke of them as laundry to be smoothed
        by the great iron
Of faith which set creases worthy of paradise. And there,
        when only
A hum came clear, they might have been speaking from clouds
        like the dead,
But what mattered when the room went dark was the voices
        reaching into
The lamp-lit living room of men who listened then, watching
        the doorway
And nodding at the nostrums offered by the tongues
        of the unseen
As if the sorrows were soothed by the lost dialect
        of the soul
Which whispered to the enormous ache of the imminent.

# The Horns of Guy Lombardo

Because I am ten years old and unashamed,
Because I've played the trombone for a year
And can read songs from a book of standards,
I walk off our porch to play Auld Lang Syne
At midnight to my family's applause.

My parents must know that a year from now
I will refuse to play for our neighbors,
But this is how we spend the first two minutes
Of 1956, the year before
I worried about sex and God's absence.

I am as confident as the flood light
That illuminates the black, simple notes
And casts shadows so dark on the driveway
I can see the slide extend and retract
Like the sluggish tongue of an ancient frog.

My father is about to be thirty-eight,
His nails, even on off-days, black with work.
That evening, he knows his bakery
Will fail, groceries filling with cheap bread
And cake mixes easy enough for fools.

My mother's body is beginning to sag
With the weight of her collapsing thyroid
And the heavy numbers of blood pressure,
But she smiles and begins to sing the words
Like someone who expects to recover.

The snow, I imagine, is softening
My tone, making me sound as mellow as
The horns of Guy Lombardo, what the rest
Of the world kisses along to unless
They have stumbled outside at midnight, close

Enough to catch my song, hearing something
Like resolutions flung into the air.

## False Dawn

My father shook me from sleep to say "Look,"
Directing me east toward a cone of light.
I thought he meant me to know the H-bomb
Had finally fallen, that our campground
Was fortunate to be a hundred miles
From Pittsburgh, even farther from New York,
The city I guessed was first to explode.
I stared at the end of the world, waiting
For him to explain what would follow, and
Because there was no moon, that glow faded
To the first question I managed, thinking
Radiation, "How far away was that?"
"How far away is the sun?" he answered,
Sounding so symbolic I expected
To be dead that day until he added,
"Now you can say you've seen something special."
At five a.m., I lay awake, telling
Myself there was a baseball game of time
Until sunrise, one inning already
Ended, the second started by strikeout.
"It's space debris," he murmured in the dark,
And I imagined the small particles
Of Earth drifting toward somebody who knew,
Like my father, what false dawn was, how dust
Could glow when aligned in the moonless night.
School would soon begin in Pittsburgh, still there,
And Miss Bell would elaborate, for sure,
On the canals of Mars, what she had taught
My sister the year before, how Martians
Had been so smart their incredible work
Could be seen from millions of miles away,
Yet they had vanished like the dinosaurs.

## White Gloves

Going out meant church, my mother,
Like a surgeon, slipping on white gloves
At the door. They said she was ready;
They said get in the car, sit in back,
And remember, keep the window up.

She held a tissue to the handles
And knobs between our house and our pew.
She wore them once and washed them; she owned
A second, identical pair,
Three ridges along the back that matched

The two pair in boxes she'd wear new
For Easter or Christmas or weddings
That requested extended hands.
White gloves, she said, were like glasses,
What she needed to see past herself.

The President's beautiful wife wore
White gloves like lipstick, her newsreel hands
Bleached by public expectation,
But after Dallas, my mother
Entered her Sundays without them.

She prayed with her fingers touching
Until only old women were white
To the wrists, and she died, three pair
In the drawer of her last things, two pair
Waiting in boxes like the souls

Of the unborn, so patient, so long,
They were lamps left on when the day
Enters through windows, light unnoticed
Until evening when we're surprised
And say to ourselves, remember.

# The 1918 House

My father, whose limp is a stutter,
Says he was born in the epidemic,
The early days, when people survived
As expected because it was just flu.

In May, he tells me, the cases were
Three day fevers. By June, he says, the flu
Had moved to where it always summers,
Far from the warm weather of families.

My father, who shuffles like those who
Are stared at by children, accepts my hand
For surfaces other than sidewalks
To examine every place where he's lived.

In September, he tells me, symptoms
Meant death--the coughing of blood, the blue face,
The darkening of feet that said "soon"
In the common language for conclusion.

The lungs, he says, went soggy with blood,
The people drowned for days. The newly born,
He murmurs, were passed over like sons
Of Jews, God's mercy on our infant breath.

My father, who refuses a cane,
Touches a wall he built in a yard owned
By strangers, pausing on his way to
The beginning, the house where, in the year

Of the Spanish flu, he was first-born
And no one died; where his parents survived
To see themselves chosen, praising God
And good fortune and their lifetimes of work.

On both sides, he says, are the houses
Of victims, sons who enlisted for war,
And he pauses, the porch so different
I have to read the number to prove it.

How winter blessed us, he says, ending
That horror, driving us inside to love.
He asks me to knock on the white door;
He says these people will invite us in.

## The Pause in the Plummet for Prayer

They'd plunged thousands of feet, crash-certain, and now,
Miles above the Pacific, a passenger
Walked the aisle like a stewardess. Let us pray,
She said, and believers, those passengers did,
Filling the unexplainable nine minutes
Of frail stability with supplication.
That plane scribbled like a toddler on the sky
While every one of them felt saved, we're told, Flight
Two Sixty-one's miracle joining the best
Stories that begin, "Did you know?" passed forward
By the bucket brigade of word-of-mouth, and
Emptied, sent back by the living, retraced from
Here to there to witnesses who cannot speak.

No matter the disaster stories we hear
And repeat, a marvel of wishes spreads from
Our words--healings, sightings, the necessary
Resurrections growing like the hybrid tree
We planted--in seven years, the tallest thing
On our street; in seven more so enormous
We took it down, and yet it drives a thousand
Descendants from roots spread the length of our yard.
Our neighbors walk out to a field of saplings
Sprung up like gifts from the magi of desire.
This morning, standing among them, we marvel
At the force of rebirth, how, if everything
Returned, we would stand in the darkness of awe.

*Reviving the Dead* (2011)

# Telling the Bees

*In old England, after a death, family members
went to the nearest beehive to tell the bees.*

My father, at eighty-nine, abandoned
His yard to hired help and neglect. He drew
His bedroom drapes as if he were closing
That theater like a bankrupt business.

He opened, one morning, those year-closed drapes
And saw, astonished, a wasp nest grown huge
Under the eaves, something to watch instead
Of the television he could not hear.

He followed that window's feature each day,
The silent movie of work, the mute slap
Of small bodies on glass, and though it is
A custom to which I give no credence,

And though they're not even the bees of myth,
I work my way among the Rose of Sharon
Planted, years ago, as fence, and offer
My reason for visiting, come to choose

Photographs as keepsakes after the death
I announce to the busy air like someone
Superstitious enough to think the words
I use must be understood by the deaf.

# Dust

Missing the ride that ended in wreckage,
A friend's mother dead where I would have sat,
I remembered his dashboard St. Christopher,
The rosary beads that draped it as double
Insurance for loss. I spent an evening
Reading about relics, splinters of ark
And cross, the shrouds of the saintly, holy bits
And pieces that signified paradises
Made possible by faith and ignorance,
Circumstance, chance, all of them, yesterday,
Reduced to wishes under the Imax dome
Where the Hubble photographs demonstrated
The enormity of dust while my friend
Strained to find representation for faith.
So near his lost comfort, the heavens became
A billion suns where surely someone worships
While elsewhere someone suffers the terror
Of understanding. A voice recited
In light-year language, the vocabulary
For endlessness, yet my friend threw his head back
To absorb the Pillars of Creation,
Those famous nebulae, and I listened,
Beside him, to the theory of dark matter,
Eighty per cent of the universe ascribed
To the utterly transparent darkness
Of the unobservable, hearing him
Murmur the brief acquiescence of amen,
The lenses of our eyes enhanced to the scope
Of gods who, knowing the unaccounted for,
Turn their flimsy backs to the expanding dust.

## The Beheaded

Some scientists, this week, claim there was time
Before the Big Bang, citing evidence
That shrinks the cheap shirts of our lives until
Our bellies are revealed like perversions.
It's enough to reconsider the time
Before the Big Bang of our conceptions,
The world at ease with our absence, taking
Its ordinary time through centuries,
None of them ending in apocalypse,
No one rising from graves but characters
In stories, and yet I'm thinking about
The brutal contractions of loneliness,
Its extraordinary, unheard screaming
Before the wailing of what's become us.

My student, just yesterday, insisted
We'd recognize our beheaded bodies
As long as forty seconds, sufficient
For understanding. An insomniac,
She tells me she can see her sleepless self
The way the beheaded watch their bodies.
Such sight comes with wakefulness, she explains,
Her body prone for hours like a patient
Etherized, yet awake, one more story
I've read, someone hearing a surgeon speak
The soft, private language of hopelessness.

Or this common story, my father's place,
This afternoon, among the nearly dead
In a room with a door that doesn't lock.
He's wrapped in flannel shirt and two sweaters,
Each buttoned to the throat while the heat hums
From every baseboard as he takes his pulse
Each hour, expecting to hear, I'm sure,

The incredible first silence of stopped.
I wheel him to the window he purchased
Thirteen years ago, the stained-glass mural
For my mother nearly a decade dead,
And he recognizes nothing until
I set him inches from her name and his,
Saying "read every word" like a teacher,
Already looking back on my visit
As it topples headless into the past.

How the world ripens without us, how mouths
Welcome its beauty and we are sorely
Unmissed, becoming spirit or nothing
But a generation's occasional
Remembering. And yet we are able
To answer annihilation with names
That science hasn't slaughtered; not yet, not
If we refuse to relinquish the love
That extends our moments by embracing.

# Evaluation

Overhearing, in a bar, a student
Declare my poems conservative, line
By syllabic line, I sat myself small.
Art is such a pretty thing, she prattled,
And more important, unfathomable.
Nothing could be truer than mystery.
Writers had used commas for centuries.
Enough of that, and enough of letters
In upper case, time arranged by verb tense.
Conventional spelling? Why so stuffy?
And forget about syntax that travels
The worn path of clarity. When nouns fail,
There are coinages; when verbs seem frail, drop
Hyphens between two like beautiful yokes.

There were mixed drinks scattered nearby, the kind
That feature flavored vodka, two liqueurs,
And small splashes of tropical juices
Sparkling in sugary combinations.
The bartender, because she's an artist,
Makes them only once. The bowl-sized glasses
Confirmed it, the color otherworldly
As the cloudless heavens above Xyrgyst,
The seventh planet from a pair of suns.
Across from me a man nursed beer in which
A plum slice swam like an exotic fish,
His mug an aquarium to admire,
And I heard pentameter spit loudly,
Narrative shouted like a blasphemy,
Regardless of suffering or who loves
Alone, the reliably ordered heart
Voicing its rhythmic, conventional needs.

## For Good

He's dead and gone, and yet you read
That a man in Serbia has
Driven a stake into the grave
Of Slobodan Milosevic,
As if superstition has not
Been domesticated to flags
And flowers, as if you might walk
To the gravesites of those you hate
In order to spike the soil
And repeat, three times, "For good."
As if you might haul that stake home
In the trunk of your car, something
To keep in the garage among
The garden tools, the grave's earth dried
And caked upon its brittle point.
In early March, you hammer it
Into the ground among a bed
Of perennials; throughout April,
You examine the earth, and when
Every bud reappears you weep
And carry that stake inside where
There's a place for it by your bed,
Your hand reaching for it each time
The darkness speaks its dialect
Of shame, holding its point over
Your heart to coerce a symbol,
The Milosevic of yourself
As adamant as April while
You rehearse like a citizen
Of a tiny theocracy
Where consolation can be held
Like a stark, sacred affliction.

## Scattering

From six to ten pounds, our cremains
Will weigh, the visible fragments
White or gray, the largest pieces
Ground to sand-size for discretion
And the ease of our scattering.

Not comforting, this summary,
But better, pre-need, than the one
Describing decomposition
By traditional burial.

Better yet, post-burning options
Carry romance for the living—
Etched keepsake urns, ash-speckled cards,
Jewelry that carries cremains
Near the wrists, the throat and the heart.

Carry ceremony, as well—
Scatterings at sea, in meadows,
Off cliffs or the small balcony
Of the dead's high-rise apartment,

Because height, most often, is craved—
From airplanes, from helicopters
And hot-air balloons, even from
The raised barrel of a shotgun
To ensure a high arc of dust.

And lately, fireworks, with music,
Those ashes blown into rainbows
To ooohs and aaahs from the living,
Bringing to mind what's new, the launch

Into space, the years-long orbit
Until small meteors of ash
Plummet again into burning.
And now there are those who will pay
For lift-off to the moon and Mars,

The beautiful, infinite ride
Beyond solar system borders,
Escaping, they convince themselves,
The great scenario of ash,

How the Earth, in a billion years,
Will become a planet of dust;
How, finally, it will spiral
Into the huge, expanding sun,
Which, while dying, will scatter Earth

As if it needed to render
All of our cremains to swirling
In eternal memorial,
Perfecting grief, at last, because

There's never enough preserving,
Never enough remembering
As we fling those we love in wide,
Then wider arcs, as if distance
Can photograph the dead, create

An image we're able to see
When we're alone, concentrating
On some speck of sky as we breathe
The heavenly dust of the loved.

# Translating the Hawk

For three days, the hawk perches on our roof's peak, at the west end where it overlooks my wife and me on our deck, from where it can swoop down and reach us with its claws and beak before we leave our chairs. Each day are hours of absence ended by flight we follow because we sit outside and wait as if the sky were television, the hawk a program filmed exclusively for us. We feel changed beneath it, August curling shut, brittle with heat. We celebrate the guest we do not speak to, whatever it sees in us staying secret as death. And though we cannot name it, narrowing by color and size, we believe it a male who returns because we wait, the hawk on the house a yoke of used time we gladly shoulder, the hawk making us rise before dawn, our doors left open all night because we want our emerging to be silent, just the screen's soft shuffle outward and back, the hawk, three times, exactly where we left him, his evenings a story he will tell us when we learn to translate the silence the way we have learned to interpret God, what he might be saying from another world which can only be reached through flight.

*The History of Permanence* (2011)

## The Possibilities for Wings

How often have the customs of strangers
Silenced me into dreaming their beliefs.
In Java, for example, some people
Insist the souls of suicides return
In the bodies of crows, while in Scotland,
Souls of the lonely flee to butterflies.

In Pennsylvania? In this town where death
Belongs to those with names I've said, the souls
Of the ordinary are cries called out
And gone into an afternoon of rain,
Leaving me to wish winged things for the friend
Whose heart has failed, the friend who killed himself
In his meticulously sealed garage.

In my back yard? I'm talking to the friend
Who, like me, has sidestepped the terrible,
And even, from time to time, laughs aloud,
Neither of us, not yet, fluttering off
In moths or whatever we might predict
For our futures, the possible wings for
Depression, jealousy, the waste of hours.

Choose one? he asks, and I say the poorwill,
The only bird that hibernates, waking,
After months, to flight. Yes, he answers, good.
Overhead, just now, a small plane pierces
The air, and I imagine both of us
On board, becoming birds that seem to fly
Without love of anything but ourselves,
Shaping our fear against the summoned sky.

## The Serious Surprise of Sorrow

She's twelve, the girl who discovers a foot
Washed ashore in British Columbia,
Interviewed, she chatters, puzzled, amazed.

Attention is an awkward thing, she thinks,
And now she's been chosen as the witness
To the arrival of a miracle

Because two more feet, both left, like the one
She found, have landed on nearby beaches,
All of them wearing size-12 running shoes

Like a tiny cluster of rare cancer.
Surely, they had mates, though left and right feet
Respond differently to the sea's currents,

According to the oceanographer
Who tracked, once, the paths of rubber ducks spilled
From a ship like a flotilla for joy.

Somewhere, then, the shoed right feet are floating
Toward another country, size-12 men
Targeted like unbribable judges.

Those feet will wash up on a thousand blogs;
Those feet will litter the crowded beaches
Of a million chat room conversations

Until time's incinerator turns them
To ash, becoming the urban legend
Of the wilderness that always concludes

With a girl who still believes that three men
Are limping somewhere on the prosthetics
For impossible chance, not already

Eaten by the grim mouths of the ocean,
That chosen girl growing into knowing
There is no limit to what we are asked

To accept, giving a personal name
To the serious surprise of sorrow,
Unable to stop scanning like those men

From our town's senior center who carry
Metal detectors to the nearby park,
Walking with stuttering steps like robins,

Their heads cocked a moment, then cocked again,
Their beaks passing over the unmown grass,
Listening for the soil's faintest sound.

## After the Aberfan Disaster

*On Oct. 21, 1966, in Wales, an 800-foot-high "tip" of rock, coal, mud, and shale collapsed, crushing an elementary school, killing 116 children and five teachers.*


In this story, the assembled children
Have just sung "All Things Bright and Beautiful."
In this story, a survivor recalls
"In that silence, you couldn't hear a bird,"
The slag thirty feet deep, a certainty.

In this story, the crushed children are called
By their parents. In this story, so few
Of them answer they become miracles,
The kind where ten lepers are cleansed, leaving
A colony of others to fester.

In this story, the children are smothered
By indifference, the company's and mine,
Because I am cowering from the draft,
Only college between me and combat.
That afternoon, I drive my father's car

One hundred miles per hour on a road
With a dozen intersections, and slow,
Trembling, into the sudden afterward
Of my brief, self-made miracle, thinking
What else proves I belong to the future?

Those children and their teachers are as dead
As two friends killed in cars. Some minister,
Days later, repeats, "In all things, design"
In a sermon I overhear, sounding
As if he's casting a blessing on rape.

A half mile from that service are slag heaps
High enough to take the light an hour
Early each evening. This story has me
Cautiously climbing each one with a friend
Soon to be blown apart in Vietnam.

Could there have been an alternate story
To the one I was breathing behind him?
So safely enrolled, who had I become
But a patient with purchased remission,
Reading about loss in expensive rooms?

## Selflessness

In the animal kingdom, among fish,
one father carries all of the laid eggs
in his mouth, sixty-five-day starvation
to make that flexible, deep mouth a womb.

Such sacrifice, spitting them out at last,
following that fast with the daily chores
of parenting: to guard them while they feed,
to take them back into his mouth like God.

Those babies need to grow before something
hungry finds them. They need a place to sleep
safe enough to wake again to feeding,
watched carefully by their selfless father.

He's a living prayer, that catfish who knows
each child as he opens his mouth for them.
Though every father has limits, and so
does this one, turning his back, one morning,

as they feed, swimming away while he still
knows them, before his children grow so large
he can't tell them from what he hungers for.
If he forgets to flee, he will eat them.

# The Dead Girls

1

The girl who martyred her dolls, sending them
To heaven to wait for her arrival,
Sentenced them to stones or fire or the force
Of her hands to tear them, methods she'd learned
From the serious, dark nuns who taught her.

She would press a pillow over my face
To encourage sainthood. "Now," she would say,
Leaning down, and I'd let myself go limp
And lie quietly for her arrangements.

Her hands clasped like Mary's in the painting
Over her bed, she prayed for my body.
Sparingly, she sprinkled me with lotion.
Always, because she'd taught the proper way
To stare, my eyes were open when I died.

That summer, in the months before fourth grade,
Her uniforms waited in the closet
For September, her white communion dress
Beside them, declaring to St. Agnes,
Who watched from the sunlit, opposite wall.

In August, her mother ran a vacuum
Through the house, moving from the living room
Of St. Francis to the narrow hallway
Of Our Lady of Lourdes, and I stayed dead

Until the sound reached that girl's room, rising
To her mother's clenched roar of cleanliness,
Both of us keeping our feet off the floor,
Giving her a swipe of room to work, clearing
The way for temporary perfection.

2

The girl who loved to be touched in cemeteries,
Who said the dead reminded her to ecstasy,
Offered her body to my hands while I agreed,
Thanking the lost for their shadowed grove of headstones.

Always it was dark or nearly so, that girl shy
About her disrespect or nakedness, until,
At last, approaching cemeteries in weak light
Made me want to fuck above a thousand strangers.

One night, accidentally, the death of someone
Both of us knew, someone our age, meaning nineteen.
The violence of loss a lump underneath us
No matter which well-tended garden we entered.

Though frankly, we were exhausted by then, tired
Of each other's needs, and the dead could do nothing
Except talk among themselves about our absence,
Using the inaudible language of the earth.

3

The girl who died the following day
Is still talking in my car. She sits
Beside me, knees drawn up to her chin
Like a pouting child. Expectation
Is the only thing that will happen
Between us, the car's radio full
Of the British Invasion until
I follow her under the driveway's
Double floodlights to the house I will
Never be inside. "Next week," she says,
Before I drive past where she will die
In another boy's new car, the site
So often seen I notice nothing
But oncoming headlights, the bright ones
Under the influence of midnight,
The day she will die just now begun,
The radio switched to Marvin Gaye
And James Brown, the road so familiar
I can be careless with attention
As I speed toward the unexpected,
What weekends are for, story makers.

# Things That Fall from the Sky

*Seeds*

Take one early evening. A father calls
His wife and children outside to witness
The eastern sky going bloody with clouds.
"What?" they say, transfixed, "what?" staring skyward
Until the rain swarms like sand, a brief storm
Of seeds that spreads them apart, their eyes closed
Under this brief anomaly of hail.

The after-light is so yellow it seems
To have traveled here from a jaundiced star.
Before he can speak, the father must kneel
To examine that rain, his wonder turned
Watery, doubt taking his fingertips
Over their pinpricked skin to read the Braille
Of what might be born from a vocal rain.

A name for the first day of invasion
Wells up in him, a long vowel that leaves
Its breath on their faces. When they watch him
Like babies, that man smiles the first falsehood
Of devotion, afraid they already
Believe so much in these seeds, they'll swallow,
Certain that superstition will feed them.

*Powder*

> *In 1969, in South Carolina, nondairy creamer from
> the new Borden plant began to fall on a small town.*

1

The day became white and sweet
Like the air above a rolling pin

As a woman thins the dough
For chip-filled cookies. Children stood

Beside their mothers, their hands
Clutching toys they would not part with.

2

The weather cut the neighborhood
Into the shapes of families.

The cloud was soluble on tongues.
It surrounded each face like sound.

Already there were footprints
On sidewalks, a dream of shovels.

3

Those dusted by light took vows.
Suddenly, declarations of love,

The streets become hospitals.
Time was ending. A memory

Of old prophecies collected
In the eyes of everyone.

4

At last, the company's reassurance,
Though later, when the whitened bathed,

They stroked the film that had formed
Along their cheeks, their fingertips

Dizzy with the wonder of children
Touching the rouged faces of the dead.

*Documents*

> *In 1973, a set of papers that explained, with graphs and formulas, "normalized extinction" and the Davis-Greenstein mechanism of astrophysics, fell from a distance higher than a 300-foot radio transmission tower.*

When the papers fell from the sky, it looked
As if a briefcase had opened, a latch
Sprung loose among the clouds, spilling a set
Of documents, nothing in that story
To rush cameras right over, not when
There'd been a robbery and a fire, not when
The news desk smelled the late-night stink of hoax.

But there was the detail of the tower,
How its height was cited, and documents
Aren't a rock-format prank. Moreover,
This caller worked in radio, a sort
Of cousin to humor when he described
Formulas and graphs, suggesting a plot
Filled with spies or scientists dangerous
With political or religious hate.

A few lines then. A small item below
An ad for dishwashers, television
Running a gutted house and empty safe
As if its news were in summer reruns.
But after, when no one claimed those papers,
*Chosen* repeated itself like *amen*
As the last word of that witness' thoughts.

Prophecy, now, was physics, difficult
As a burning bush or exploding star.
And didn't "normalized extinction" sound
Like a careless spin on nuclear war?
He remembered the meteor legend,
How it explained the end of dinosaurs,

All things large starving in the dusty years
Of toxic darkness. Scholarship set in
Like the deep winter of apprehension.
Each night, before looking up, he wished for
The empty sky of the ordinary.

*Meat*

After meat fell from the sky,
After that shower ended
Like a cold tap twisted shut,
There were men who sampled it,
Cautiously chewing like kings.
Like mutton, one said, relieved,
Or venison, second choice,
Someone suggesting vultures
Had vomited together
From overhead; somebody,
At last, saying they were scraps
From God's table, calling up
The old words for mystery
That caught in the throat like bones.
The men who had eaten coughed
While wishes circulated
Like secrets pledged to silence.
For days, children examined
Their fathers for fur and claws.
Old wives were as tentative as
The child brides they had been, deep
In the nineteenth century

When transubstantiation
Was a bright, beautiful fact.
So it is with the strange.
A choir of analysts
Performed the old cantata
Of certainties until meat
Was people who had been ripped
To pieces by the sharp scythe
Of tornado, their parts swirled
Upward and returned as rain.
A family was missing.
Parables were passed through yards
Until streets of disciples
Formed a holy neighborhood.
A chattering of voices
Settled on porches, the words
So much the same they sounded
Like clouds of starlings rising.

*Bodies*

Begin with the one that famously
Landed on a San Diego car,
Dropping from a mid-air accident
Like a fantastically narrow storm.
Nothing can come from such plummeting
But disaster or the miracle
That needs snow drifts and touch downs precise
As ones that land softly on Mars, yet
The melodrama transfixes us
The way children, once, at matinees,
Were caught by serial cliffhangers
And spent a week believing rescue
As impossible as growing old.

That driver and her child were unharmed,
But afterward, she had a habit
Of glancing up like a forecaster.
Though it's rare, anyone looking up
For the descent of bodies, rarer
To believe they're falling from a cloud.
It takes the height that turns us breathless,
A thousand feet or more to make us
Think "sky" like one morning when distance
Throttled our breath while suited bodies
Plunged like drops of a passing shower
That pockmark the dust of current drought.

And I, for once, agreed on something
With my sad, conservative neighbors,
Desiring a sect of people dead,
Their lives snuffed by gene anomaly.
The body of Christ, the blood of Christ—
The chorus of communion became
The password into our side for war.
It drummed in the inner ear like pulse,
And I dreamed myself marching to plant
The first flag of a lifetime, tending
It each morning as if cloth might die
And declare me criminal and cruel
In the common carelessness of peace.

## Something to Think About

*Dying, Henry Cavendish, the reclusive scientist, ordered his servants from the room because he had "something to think about."*

*It's Something*

Who isn't taken by stories like the one
About M. Boulard, who owned seven houses,
Each of them bearing a hundred thousand books.
Or Richard Heber, who believed he needed
Three copies of every volume, eight houses
In three countries necessary to hold them.

And reading those numbers, who doesn't decide
There's likely no limit for hoarders, someone
Like Sir Thomas Phillips, who wanted the most,
Driving two wives crazy with his collection,
Intending to own every book in the world.

And lately, my neighbor, not mentioned, not yet,
In such lists, though he buys books by the thousands,
Clearing out sales from garages and front yards
To fill his basement floor to ceiling, starting,
This year, on rooms left vacant by his daughters
Grown and gone, arranging his hundred thousand
In chronological order to create,
He says, the twentieth century of books,
Including seven copies of *Blue Highways*
And six of *Road Song*, the doubles and triples
He shows me when I follow his guided tour.

Downstairs, I imagine fire; upstairs, collapse,
His house imploded by millions of pages.
I stand beside him in his daughter's bedroom,
The 90s surrounding us, and think of books
I've published, none visible upon these shelves.
Next door is the 80s, the odds long against
My earliest, and I remember searching
Bookstore shelves, drifting down the Fs, despondent.

I keep to myself that I own seventy
Of one title, thirty-five of another,
Lugging them to readings where they leak away,
Some evenings, one by one. My neighbor, standing
Where his house is clear, sweeps his large hands apart
As if he's showing me stars, the infinite
Sprawled and demanding to be seen. A second,
Then two, he holds them wide until I manage,
"It's something," backing into the driveway where
His station wagon sits low and stacked, waiting
Like a boxcar for his insatiable hands.

*Weighing the World*

Begin with Cavendish proving that water
Wasn't the element the world thought it was.
Follow that with his silence, how frightening
All women were, so unbearable to glimpse
He left notes for his housekeeper, constructing
A second staircase for her exclusive use.

Such seclusion is its own education,
The bookishness of silence teaching, subject
By subject, what haunts sufficiently to say.
An example? Cavendish, so mute, would weigh
The world by calculating its density,
Sending his proof to ordinary people
Who had learned the density of feigned friendships,
To weigh anger, disinterest, and disdain.

Now imagine Cavendish, one afternoon,
Paused at the base of the housekeeper's staircase,
That woman on errands he's put in writing.

Certain of her absence, he begins to climb,
Reaches the second floor to stand on a spot
So strange he hears the light in a foreign tongue.
Then think of the scenario for descent,
The choice, if he lingers, of her stairs or his.

Improbable? Once, during a reception,
I spent an hour alone in an upstairs room
Where I'd carried two glasses of chardonnay
Like a husband. There were books and photographs,
A bed perfectly made by the housekeeper
My university gives its president.

I sat on the one shadowed chair where his wife
Would examine herself, perhaps, before sleep,
The house beneath me so dense with my colleagues
It grew gravity that kept me from rising.
Eleven sets of footsteps passed in the hall;
Each time a toilet flushed and water ran
Before they reversed direction like sentries.

Sitting there, I had something to think about,
How all those guests would honor the promises
They'd spoken to leave solitude to others.
At last, I calculated the weight of lies
I needed to carry downstairs. I finished
That wine and placed both glasses on the table
Beside the hardbound stories of Henry James.
Regaining my feet was as hard as rising
After a week of flu. *There*, I thought, *like that*,
Hand on the polished railing and then, three steps
From the foot of the stairs, letting go, prepared.

*Competitive Eating*

Famously, this summer, sixty-eight hot dogs,
Buns included, were swallowed in twelve minutes
At Coney Island, the beach packed with people
Transfixed by that brief, marvelous appetite.

Wonders, for sure, those numbers and the workings
Of the body to accept them, a strangeness
Like the swords and fire down the throats at sideshows,
But now there's an alphabetical roster

Of records for quantity and speed, starting
With asparagus, six pounds in ten minutes,
Followed by beef tongue, bologna, burritos,
The beautiful simplicity of buffet.

Alliterations of the edible fill
The page: cabbage and candy, connoli, corn,
And the connotative mention of cow brains,
Fifty-seven of them in fifteen minutes

By the same phenom who Hoovered those hot dogs.
Matzo balls, mayonnaise, meat pies—suddenly,
The weight of eating mesmerizes like breasts,
And I remember my single fling with food,

Choosing goldfish, live ones, and betting with friends
Before taking them down with water to win
Ten dollars for a dozen in a minute,
My unrecorded record for childishness.

Look, there are mouths for stones and metal and glass,
Things to be more careful with than tamales,
No limit to what we're willing to swallow—
Paragraphs of protest, a declaration

Of love, promises, dreams. Ceaselessly, we can
Listen for our sentences washed back with spit.
If we stay quiet, holding our breath, we might
Hear the infinity of words within us.

*Steinmetz in the Canoe*

Where he loved to work, using
A desk of boards, an office
Engineered for drifting
On a man-made pond.
So why shouldn't Steinmetz look
Satisfied, even healthy,
Not crippled like he appears
In that famous photograph
With Einstein, who stands taller
And straighter and better dressed
Than Steinmetz, who all but falls
Sideways while the camera
Catches his hunchback.
It was General Electric
That sold this version of their star,
Steinmetz dwarfed by
The Nobel Laureate, and nothing now
Can undo that deep shadow,
Not even the admission,
Later, that the photograph
Is altered, that they were posed,
That day, among twenty men,
That Steinmetz, too, would doctor
Photos, placing his image
In boats with young, beautiful
Women, cloning himself, each
Couple floating on water,
Perfectly paired electrons.

*The Prophecies of Mathematics*

Not even his wife wanted to listen
To Francis Galton explain that prayer made
No difference, that insurance companies
Knew the facts of longevity, and there
Was no adjustment for people who prayed
And the various buildings they lived in.
Not even, but he said it anyway—
The pious live no longer than the bad.
It's always this way with Jeremiahs.
In the prophecies of mathematics
Are equations for hours in the sun,
Alcohol in the blood, early marriage.
There, among the numbers, lies the total
Of the truth of ourselves, and I admit
I've counted the daily steps from my house
To my office through six possible routes;
I've counted the frequency of letters,
Rooting for underdogs like b and k
To outdo their predicted sums of use.

Trivial? Stupid? I estimated
The minutes, once, until the end of school,
Wrote seventy-five thousand, six hundred,
In my September notebook and followed
The lurch of each long minute on the clock
For three periods of world history,
Latin, and plane geometry until
I rejoined the classroom of common sense,
Abandoning the women who number
The knocks on a door to seven, the breaths
Before starting their cars to six, knowing
Nothing about the habits of Galton,
Who kept track of boredom by numbering
The small fidgets of a congregation,

Who counted the brush strokes as his portrait
Was painted, who evaluated place,
At last, by the beauty of its women,
Selecting London like a pageant judge,
Leaving it to us to tally the days
Till what's longed for may or may not arrive,
Keeping calendars of Xs that end,
Each time, on the eve of possible joy
Like a merciless cliffhanger for faith.

*Hypergraphia*

Early in a paperback on genius,
The chapter about the unrecognized,
Geoffrey Pyke makes ice indestructible
By adding perfect amounts of wood pulp.
For battleships, he says. For victory.
Proven, his World War II idea floats
Unused, while conventional fleets succeed.
Years of this, the unrealized, proposing
To the skeptical, each day statistics
And silenced projections, writing until,
With all that time saved by working in bed,
Not wasting hours of rising and dressing,
He proves the insomnia of despair.
His last night, for once clean-shaven, he looks
As ordinary as the generals
Who half-listened. He swallows pills and writes.
He empties a bottle and keeps writing,
Furious with final words while they turn
As illegible as the last sentence
In my A-student's suicide blue book.
Her detail of pills. Her apology.
"I don't want a scene," she wrote, flinging me
Down the sunlit hall to save her, nothing

Like my mother's clear script the day she died,
Writing, "I've never felt so nauseous,"
Fearing her kidneys failed. And after that?
Not a word about prayer, her remedy
For sin and sickness and disappointment.
She wrote about the bowl game my father
Was watching because Pittsburgh was playing.
She wrote a paragraph about Christmas,
A sentence about her fatigue and pain.
She must have made my father, at half time,
Walk that one-page letter to the mailbox
And flag it for delivery because
It lay among tax forms and catalogues
When I returned, after her funeral,
To open a week of mail, her mercy
Of words introducing eternity.

*Ferris*

For sure, there were worries—
That the wheel wouldn't turn,
That terrible weather
Would topple that thing or
Passengers uproot it
By shifting to one side.
So when summer's worst storm
Approached, Ferris gathered
His wife into the wind,
Rotating up, assured
As angels while the rest
Of Chicago rode
With the reporter
Who needed to prove
A city to the storm,
Lifting into the sky

Like a disciple
Of the machine age,
Ascending into
The windswept chill
Of survival, recording
That astonishing circle
Like a new testament,
Speaking the buoyant
Language of re-entry.

*Sticktoitiveness*

What do we want, tourists at strange sites
Like Leedskalnin's coral furniture
Within and without his house of stone?
Here is the rock home for the three bears,
Goldilocks-guests testing beds and chairs,
Believing, for now, in the porridge
Of a stranger's imagination.
Here, the first secret is work alone;
The second, persistence, all of us
Waking to impossible bodies
Of our own, the ones, if they last, that
Will spend years untouched, moving about
Like stone, heavy and hard, dependent
On the obligations of others.

Sticktoitiveness—my father's language,
Meaning school and jobs and living a life
Of faith, citing Gutzon Borglum's long haul
On Mt. Rushmore, Korczak Ziolkowski's
Decades on the unfinished Crazy Horse,
Following forty years of labor
Through a series of photos, selecting
A stone from the pile of rubble offered

As souvenirs to tourists who marveled
And returned to their own endless tasks.

Sticktoitiveness—I've flown to China,
A place for which he has no reference,
I tell him what I've witnessed from a bus,
The collective discipline of thousands
Of men rebuilding a highway by hand,
The guide assuring our group those workers
Would finish in several years, leaving
The number to us as some of those men
Hauled stones in wheelbarrows, some wielded picks
Or leaned into spades, the broken road lined
With makeshift homes surrounded by women
And children who followed their work, putting
The paved behind them like a monument,
Moving this perseverance by the mile.

Sticktoitiveness—my father tells me
The tale of Alan Foresman, who labored
On a letter to his wife for two years,
Using more than a million words to write
That novel of thoughts. Sticktoitiveness—
Year by year, I have given my father
All of my twenty-one books, expecting
Something, receiving, in exchange, "What's next?"
As if I were Yuan K'ai, the monk who carved
A two hundred foot Buddha out of rock,
Working seventy years, working alone.

# Specificity

*For Len Roberts*

*Cause of death unknown. Had never been fatally ill before.*
—Death Certificate, 1880s

Until I was twelve, *worn out*
and *God's will* were the reasons
my relatives died, my mother
speaking like a doctor, citing
visual evidence
or unknowable matters
of faith as if each were
a diagnosis of disease.

In the King James edition
of medicine, the self-help
my grandmother relied on,
there was the finality
of dropsy, the chronic palsies,
what Jesus cured, like leprosy
and possession, the devil
imbedded in the flesh like ticks.

Before she was born? People died
from convulsions and fever,
from infancy, age and tissick,
the collective name for killers
that came with coughs, as frequent
as smallpox and grip-of-the-guts,
what the dying did, at last,
when their digestion failed.

Approximation. Guesswork.
Less of that now, the x-ray
showing the shadow that will kill us,
the blood sample spilling numbers
that count us out, each tremor
specific, a thousand names
exactly right, pinpointing
each particular way to die.

Amyloidosis, for instance,
how one friend, this week, has gone.
And now, after memorial,
after an hour of tributes
by poets who traveled hours
to eulogize, I sit with my wife
who orders a glass of Chambord
for a small, expensive pleasure
in a well-decorated room,
the possibility of happiness
surprising us in the way
hummingbirds do, stuck in the air,
just now, outside this window,
attracted to the joy of sweetness
despite the clear foreshadowing
of their tiny, sprinting hearts.

*After the Three-Moon Era* (2015)

## Calculations: A Love Poem

The billionth digit of Pi is 9,
The last month without a full moon,
February 1865—
This morning I am making a list
Of the last lines of parables
About the work of numbers, about
Calculations, marking the speed
With which blood travels, as if three feet
Per second were like the blessings
On the late workers in a vineyard
Or a son just home from living with swine.

Someone continues the division
That computes the decimals of Pi.
He is telling a story, numerals
Spilling out toward infinity,
The counting a language, a life
Beyond this one, as difficult
To believe as the number of hours
We've slept together, darkness returning
And vanishing, the moments, nightly,
Between your breaths, the hesitations
In your deep sleep; my own held breath,
Listening, and then, temporarily
Relieved, turning toward the window,
Reciting the autonomic lesson
Of your lungs that swell and shrink
At last, in rhythm, their vital
Capacity, in liters, 3.1.

# Reports

On crystal meth, pond snails are better,
tests prove, at remembering pokes
from a sharp stick. In Afghanistan,
some parents use opium to settle
their children. And there are those who board
each desire as if it were a plane
scheduled for an exotic location;
for instance, the woman on heroin
in a nearby town who, needing
a companion, began to inject
her twelve-year-old daughter while the neighbor
bartered more drugs for her preteen body.

A counselor claims the girl, fourteen now,
is healing, observation's evidence
tallied in a fat, confidential file.
Incredible, we say, reading the reports,
thinking the cringing snails must believe
they are subjects of the god of stabs
or one country's children are at peace.
But yesterday, I drove past that mother's house,
slowing to turn and pass a second time,
looking for the terrible accident
of that child. I might as well have shot
heroin, too, in mime, descending
into a few hours of virtual hell.

And this morning? A report, with photo,
on the mother's once-striking beauty,
a sidebar on how the daughter, each day,
visits her in prison. The news that snails
have been turned into tiny batteries
that can be recharged with food and rest.
And furthermore, American children,
studies show, are eating more batteries,
yet nothing makes me learn the how
of these, the when and where, the why.

## After the Three-Moon Era

*The dozen fetuses of the sand shark feed on
each other until only one is left to be born.*


1

My father sings hymns aloud,
Wakes each morning expecting
To be reborn, telling me three times
As if I'm the genie for death.
He says he hears the brothers
I never had softly talking
In the small bedroom where I slept
While not one of them was born.
They whisper, he says, about the way
He refused them, saying "never"
In the disciplined sign language
Of the rhythm method, keeping
Each of them a jealous spirit.

When he sings "In the Garden,"
I imagine those brothers,
Each day, rising to where my window
Looks out at the rhododendron
Roof-high, the peace of its curtain,
Fragments of light that testify
Like character witnesses
For weather. They move their mouths
To those hymns that are heavy
With sunrise and resurrection.
Now, in October, the house holds
The early darkness and the dry heat
Of the furnace, and my father
Repeats the chorus, raising his voice
To be heard by those unborn boys
Who wake him each morning like birds.

2

A student tells me she devoured
Her twin in the womb, a doctor
Solving that natural crime
With the spaced clues of ultrasound.

She keeps her shadow twin
Sealed inside a scrapbook
She opens on her birthday,
Leaving the photo face up

In her bedroom. For when, she says,
Her family sings around her cake.
For when their voices swell
Enough to reach her sister.

3

> *Astronomers now believe Earth once had three moons.*
> *—Harper's*

Sucked into the sun
or bullied to bits
by the one moon we love,
those other moons vanished
like glittering bracelet charms
sliding off a child's wrist,
the night sky so dim
with places where tapestries
of light might fit, the empty
expanse where those moons
waited to be seen
as beautiful sisters
thrown into the sky
by a jealous god.

4

Once, in Africa, boys ran to their teacher
To tell how their friend had accepted candy
From a stranger's hand and turned into a yam.
"There," they said, "see what's left?" and that teacher
Carried the yam to the police with care.

For thirteen days, nearby, a boy's gone missing,
Turned into nothing but a column of cars
Outside our schools, mothers in silent bunches,
Buses that transport epidemic numbers,
Their red seats emptied by the virus of fear.

Stories are told about boys vanished like time,
Yet returning like swallows. The police,
In Africa, displayed that yam and people
Flocked to see. Mothers from nearby villages
Worshipped the hope of metamorphosis,

How their lost children might have been left uneaten
By some candied stranger. If only they'd been
Transformed into things with voices; if only
They could identify themselves, prove they were
Within some object to be kept and cared for.

5

At his bakery's vacant lot,
my father talks about the missing,
citing Glenn Miller, Judge Crater,
and Amelia Earhart as
we enter the knee-high weeds.
He stands at the memory
of workbench, lays his hands

to the air and carries it
to the bank of ovens.
"Ray Gricar," I say, naming
the disappeared from my town,
his computer in the river,
hard drive removed.
He tells me my mother
is slicing bread, the cash register
behind her, the three of us
working together because
he is icing a wedding cake
just before delivery,
spiraling sweetness so thick
with sugar and lard around
the figures of the bride
and groom, no one should eat it,
trusting me to balance
the three white tiers to the car.

6

Vanishing twins may occur in as many as one of every eight multi-fetus pregnancies and may not even be known in most cases. In one study, only three of twenty-one pairs of twins survived to term, suggesting intense fetal competition for space and nutrition. In some instances, vanishing twins leave no detectable trace at birth. More than one amniotic sac can be seen in early pregnancy. A few weeks later, only one.

7

Once, my fortune came with a sequence
Of cards. Once, it lay in my palms turned up
To longevity, happiness, travel, love.
Both of the tellers were serious as priests.
Each time I mentioned nothing about how
My daughter had grown into the age
Of ultrasound, one, and then two photos
Of her yet-to-be-born stuck among cards
And snapshots and short lists of things-to-do
On my refrigerator, not telling those seers
My daughter asked not to know their sex,
Her daughters old enough, now, to study
Their early selves like scholars of pre-birth.

8

The vanished twin can die from a poorly implanted placenta, a developmental anomaly that causes major organs to fail or to be completely missing, or there may be a chromosome abnormality incompatible with life.

9

My daughter has painted a sky of chairs
That sparkle like redundant constellations.
Her heaven is moonless, the chairs, she says,
Ascending. From one side, the sky bleeds
From the wounds she imagines
On an adjacent panel, one that waits
Nearby, brilliant with light.
Her daughters dream of painting it blue,
A sun shining the chairs invisible.

10

Transformations fill the museum for the missing—
A lunch box, a ribbon, a mitten, one untied shoe.
A boy became a newspaper satchel,
A girl turned into an emptied purse.
We imagine leaves on the tongue,
Mud in the eyes, the sound of weeping
Stifled by blood in the throat.

The morning of the first milk carton child—
Etan Patz, six years old and vanished—
My own three children, ages two to seven,
Ate breakfast as if they were promises
Waiting for a kiss to revive them.

11

Simultaneously,
During the three-moon era—
The full moon of joy,
The crescent moon of anticipation,
The half-moon of mercy—
Triplets hover
Unseen above
Each late-night horizon,

## 12

*Never* arrives with his flashlight,
and you follow to the river
or the woods or the damp basement
of a half-constructed house.
In the morning, you wake
with the coffee maker
set to six a.m., its cough
driving you out of sleep
like a smoke alarm.
Now, when you talk to the air,
somebody is there.
This morning three birds fly
into the living room windows,
one of them dead in the iris,
the other two missing.
A neighbor says it's three flights
of the same bird, but you remember
the music of those thumps,
the variation of size and speed,
and you see the colors
of the missing above the trees,
shades necessary as water.
You stand beneath them, reaching,
your face upturned to spaces
they have left in the sky.

# Strangers, Falling

> *Children universally find clown wallpaper frightening and unknowable.*
> —Harper's

Each one wears the white face of deletion,
Their baggy suits so uselessly ballooned,
Their enormous shoes spread like helpless sails.
Each evening passes without knowing them,
But some are splayed sideways, skidding across
What seems to be a cloudless wind-swept sky
Some are seated on nothing, plummeting
From unseen planes. Or they're twisted, head-first,
Bright smiles lasting to the floor where their legs
Still pedal air, the child, upon waking,
Most frightened by the arms-extended clowns
Who concentrate on improbable flight.

The child asks about sky, where it begins.
At the far edge of everything, he's told,
Where clear weather is always expected.
The clowns, then, must fall from above the sun,
But some mornings he thinks they're carried up
To fall again by an anger of wind
Inside the wall where scratching lives with fright.
When he holds his mouth exactly like theirs
As he stands in his father's floppy shoes,
He feels the floor fall out from under him.
He would disappear if he held that smile;
He would know who they were as he tumbled.

## According to *Ibid*

According to *Ibid*, one student wrote,
dutifully acknowledging his frequent,
reliable source whose name suggested
an old, Roman Empire philosopher
so prolific he must have been busy
twenty-four/seven. Good Lord, this fellow
*Ibid* must have scratched out a hundred books
by the looks of it, volumes everywhere,
and so varied, what his mother pronounced
a Renaissance man, all those long hours
in libraries building reputation
until a myriad of pronouncements
could be safely attributed to him.

When he had time, he'd Google *Ibid*, but
there must be a million hits for someone
he'd cited in English and history,
in sociology and art, *Ibid*
so wise he fortified every thesis.
What's more, he'd learned that even *Ibid* had
second thoughts, research rushing over him
like floodwater until he constructed
a safe, new raft of evidence so huge
that whole papers could be a paraphrase
of Ibid, so famous now he was known
by only one name like Bono and Sting,
Madonna and Prince, or any of those
Brazilian soccer players who have been
reverently cited as if their shirts were
emblazoned with the signatures of gods.

# The History of Fail-Safe

So tightly coiled, the new way to say, "point of no return" became a spring.

We repeated the word with reverence.
We knew what cursing this God could bring us.

Its Bible backed into our lives, tail lights blinking,
then darkening, its make and model mystery.

Hymns were written, all of them prayers that no one sang,
afraid they would lead our fear into temptation.

Our locks were the kind with extended bolts.
Inside our shelters, we slid the short chains
into the slots that sighed reassurance.

Somebody whispered, "Mutual assured destruction."
"What?" we asked. "What?" But the phrase lay dormant in our blood
with the necessary poisons we breathed and swallowed.

We studied Latin's declensions, the inflected
endings for case. In May, we wore togas to class.
The Romans had worshipped gods dressed like us. To learn
Russian would have shown the world we were terrified.

When the Conelrad scream spilled from our speakers,
we counted to twenty, anticipating
*This is not a test.* "Now," our teacher told us,
"everybody knows what it's like to be old."

The old yearbooks were nostalgic with mustard gas
and artillery; they joked about hand-to-hand.
The seniors, for homecoming, carried stones and clubs.
The juniors slung bows and arrows across their backs.
The youngest students armed in another building.

In the stadium, in the fourth quarter,
all the coaches listened to the chugging
of the two-word cheer. The line of scrimmage
dug a trench into the turf. Strategy
was born through the C-section of evening.

While we celebrated in the gymnasium,
apprehension crawled underground in Nevada.
After it disappeared, everyone could still see
its fat ass squirm, indelible as the landscape.

Stand-off was playing on the radio again,
an oldie already, as dated as doo-wop.
We pointed at the sky like toddlers, our fingers
forming the weapons with which we conquered playgrounds.

Fail-Safe turned so red, it glowed like a sore.
Fail-Safe sat in bars until closing time.
Fail-Safe grew fat, breathed heavy on the stairs.

One morning we felt dizzy and our speech began
to fail. When we sat down, starting over, we lost
our legs to the polio of uncertainty.

Every pilot tested the scarred-white wrists of the future. Their
instruments explained precisely where they were, about to say "When."

When the insects emerged, when there were
no shoes and beaks in their baffling skies,

they chittered and squealed among themselves
as if alarm had left their language

since science had briefly entered them.

## The Illiterate in New Mexico

After I failed calculus, my father,
A maintenance man, asked me if I knew
The story of how janitors were hired
In Alamogordo, New Mexico,
Whether the name of that town meant something
Or if I'd stopped thinking altogether
About anything but my present self.
"F," he hurled, "is your failure," and I said,
"The atomic bomb" before he shouted,
"If you couldn't read a word, you were hired,
An illiterate in New Mexico."

We were together in a restaurant.
I was as old, within days, as the bomb
And was supposed to become a doctor,
Not clean up after their accomplishments,
Somebody who'd never know their secrets,
A failure sweeping up in ignorance.
All I'd ever be was a patient; all
I'd be able to do was listen while
The way my life would close was decided,
An illiterate in New Mexico.

The scientists, he said, were creating
The end of the world while those janitors,
Excluded from their secrets, emptied trash.
Lips moving, he calculated a tip
Before sliding three quarters and two dimes
Under his plate, waiting for me to stand,
Leaving my grades open on the table
Because I needed to understand that
Anyone, even a goddamned busboy,
Could recognize I was as helpless as
The illiterate in New Mexico.

*The Infinity Room* (2018)

## Distraction Therapy

To manage fear, start anywhere
and count backwards by threes and eights.
Or multiply—the times tables

can soothe the heart. To slow breathing,
tap your feet. Do knee bends. If you
hum melodies, you will believe

you're dancing. To stop panic,
try anagrams or spell the names
for where you are. Find all the words

within them. Keep track of your score.
To break anxiety, focus
on something far in front of you.

Walk toward it, totaling your steps.
To resist the next bad moment,
press one hand into the other.

To handle the next after that,
grip them tight and begin to pull.
The hands are antidotes. Pit left

against the right. Feel that? Each time
you fight yourself, you smother fear.
To keep from dying, remember

the times you've survived. That list holds
all the terrors you imagine.
Read them aloud. Then breathe. Then breathe.

## During the Retirement Semester

My students, in unison, say they are
veterans of school lockdowns, that we meet
in a room as exposed as a hostage.
They have friends abroad in Paris, ones who
ordered a safe, early dinner inside
the terrorists' selected restaurant.
When Marlena says she hopes her shooter
is a woman who believes in something,
the class agrees there is nothing stranger
than sacrificing a life for faith, and
because we are inside a rectory
refurbished for our workshops, or because
they're young, I say that a girl I once kissed
declared she was saving herself for . . . then
paused and looked away as if the object
of her soft preposition was close by,
that who she became was a former nun,
thirty years and leaving as if she'd been
waiting for retirement's full benefits,
that she laughed easily and lived alone
in a studio apartment she cramped
with wall-length shelves of holy replicas.
None of them remember seeing a nun,
even the two who were raised Catholic,
and they chatter about obsolescence,
cheery with distraction, barely younger
than the archivist who had asked me, just
before class, what audience I believed
had interest enough to examine

what I'd boxed and filed. Extraordinary,
she said, her voice emptying my office,
the door, off plumb, nearly closing itself
behind her as if, inside that former
bedroom of priests, privacy was powered
by some forgotten relic they'd once shown
to their housekeepers, aging nuns who lived
below them in half the space, their comfort
sacrificed for the artless needs of God.

## The Earth, We're Told, Is Humming

Beneath our feet, we're told, the ground
is always moving. Plates that shift,
continental, oceanic,
the water above creating
chorus as it rises and falls
with the moon. That hum, moreover,
is sometimes audible, a low
murmur that keeps a few of us
awake. Torture, one woman says—
headaches, nosebleeds, insomnia
following the gifted like plagues.

Now somebody records this hum
and broadcasts it online from Maine.
Speeded and amplified, he claims,
the sound is what a fetus hears
in the womb, citing how children
sitting near his speakers curl in
on themselves, how adults weep through
humming nightmares, how this monster
under the bed is the bleak groan
of instability seeping
up like badly buried waste. But

now, this morning brings the story
of the spadefoot toad that burrows
deeply beneath the desert. That
half-sleeps for weeks or even months
while listening for the sound of
a raindrop on the sand above.
Sometimes years, it takes, for that drop
to multiply sufficiently
to prompt that toad to claw its way
to a downpour, sounding its song
of desire for other toads who
have heard the rain and risen. Now,

the toads will synchronize their calls,
communal voice necessity.
Alone and singing, those toads are
easy prey, but bunched in chorus
they are safe, not because of strength,
but because coyotes will not
attack a swarm and owls require
a single target, all those eyes
and ears alert for toads designed
to ravage them one at a time
when they emerge from this earth so
sensitive it transmits the time
to sing our songs of endurance.

## Shadowing the Gravedigger

Because I have asked him, I am
In the gravedigger's truck waiting
For a funeral to finish.
To show respect, I am wearing
My best topcoat to cover jeans.
There is a distance named discrete,
And he maintains it for his job.
He never plays the radio.

The gravedigger says there are times
He shovels by hand for infants
And the cremated, holes too small
For the spade of machinery.
For those, weather is important,
The earth, if frozen, is a bitch.

Below zero, it was, the day
My mother was buried, backhoe
Visible on a nearby rise,
Mound of earth covered by something
Designed to look like summer sod.
The pastor worked January
Into meaning, snow and zero
Entwined like the benevolent
Grasp of God until we performed
The chilled amen of erasure.

My sister, four hours from here,
Stores mementoes of our parents—
A pressed dark suit, a Sunday dress.
Alone in her house, I've opened
Her bedroom closet like a thief.
Just what does she anticipate?
To dress them for judgment the way
She prepared them for burial?
I have alibis for missing
Tenderness. Yes, I was elsewhere.

Once, I say, I watched as an urn
Was laid into a grave behind
A local church. The woman's one
Surviving son shoveled soil
While the minister recited
A prayer we could follow along
The page of a printed program.

The gravedigger watches the crowd
For the retreat to cars. He talks
Over the premonition that
Insists like a tinnitus shriek.
A child must be more difficult
Than a baby, I try, and he
Says he's opened and closed the earth
For his father; now his mother
Has entered hospice. I cannot
Fill in the silence. Whatever
You can bear, he says, and we do.

## Assessing the Dead

When Gettysburg's dead, years buried,
were unearthed for removal
to national cemeteries,
someone was hired to separate
Union from Confederate.
Relying, at first, upon
jacket color, he made certain
the loyal were rewarded.

My sister, twice, has studied
photographs to perfect display,
learning which necklace our mother
wore with her blue, Sunday-only
lace-trimmed dress, how, exactly,
our father's awards were arranged
for ceremony when he put on
his scoutmasters uniform,
placing those reframed portraits
alongside both coffins like
mirrors or proof of love.

For the difficult cases,
uniform color unknown,
the grave-shifter was taught
to recognize the brand names
of shoes and the quality
of underwear to mark bones
qualified for respected graves.

And now we've learned elephants
investigate the bones of their dead
by smell and touch, using the tips
of their trunks to caress what's left.
And yes, sometimes the young can
identify their parents,
lingering longer to inspect,
or, we like to imagine,
reflect. And whether saddened
or comforted by the ordeal
of recollection, they examine
the contours of the whitened skull.
Which is how reverie begins.
Then how it ends in turning away,
the necessary going on.

# The Startling Language of Shriveling Leaves

This week, three socks slip into unpaired comas,
Sleep with the clean and useless in drawers
While the cryonists have flown in like angels.

We sat rapt through their singing, the cantatas
Of our chilled cells repaired, one by one,
Mutinied to health and youth by computer.

Our old photographs are bleeding like icons.
They are listening while we compare
The ransom demands of resurrections.

Look here, I murmur this morning, pulling off
The just-widened highway. A white sock,
A brown, a blue—they are enough to stir us

To trust walk, no other laundry for miles,
As if someone has seeded the shoulder
To set us to searching like test mice.

We watch boredom's scenery—cinders, tar,
Roadside weeds indecipherable as deeds,
And wish for small skeletons, ruptured bodies,

And flattened fur. You declare nothing should be
That laundered, not even the highway
Upon which only official tires have spun.

An arm's length swath of green-going-brown follows
The guardrail where the county has sprayed.
Sumac collapses. The poison ivy burns.

Together we listen until we hear
The startling language of shriveling leaves
And the careful chorus of our clothing.

# The Secret City

*Ed Westcott was the 29th employee hired for the Manhattan Project in Oak Ridge. He was the official photographer there from 1942 to 1966.*

Photo #1: The Perennials of Oak Ridge

The trellises are handmade, vines
And branches trained upward, beauty
And comfort compatible, though
Temporary and brief like each

Sad emphasis on hope no one
Speaks of until privacy returns.
Inside laboratories, riddles
Whispered, answers unsolvable

As the equation for heaven.
The stems climb their small increments
Of reassurance, leaves opening
To drink up the light like addicts.

Annuals have been abandoned
Like promises of surrender.
In this second summer, fast-climbing
Perennials. Possible, now, to

Believe in the sensuality
Of shadows cast by the rise of roses,
The ascension of morning glories,
Or, at least, the small contentment

Of latticework that amplifies
The spell of early evening before
Descending light diffuses into
The indifferent drift to darkness.

*Always, throughout the war, the flawless guards demand photo IDs, no exceptions.*

Photo #2: Santa Claus Arrives at Oak Ridge

Santa's made the trip by automobile.
He's working day-shift, the reindeer pastured,
But his Chevrolet is stopped like a spy's.
Although Santa ho-hos, the guards remain
In character, serious as war while
They rummage through two sacks, reminding him
The red flag of his baggy suit requires
A pat-down, including his shiny boots.

He's scuffling now, stumbling like a hobo,
That sack unwieldy with stocking stuffers,
Footing uncertain on the unpaved street
As irregular as pieces of coal
Meant to terrify the worst brat polite.
By the time he's surrounded by children
He's a mess of mud splatter, gasping brief
White clouds like the ones the reindeer pant when
The sleigh is miraculously loaded.

Housewives on Saturdays, the mothers have
Made an hour among their chores. They've dressed
For Santa Claus, the secret work of war
Set aside like a long novel, the place
Bookmarked by a small child's crayoned drawing—
The stick figures of family and pets,
An oval sun whose beams strafe house and yard.

Near Santa's hardback throne, consequence lifts
Like tentative fog; the children form lines
From the left and right, loud but orderly.
The mothers retreat. Cameras taboo,
They memorize the scene like poetry:

The bright marathon of wishful thinking,
Footballs and bicycles, dolls and board games,
Roller skates and air-rifles and all those
Perfectly detailed model air force planes.

>  *Six beauty shops, two bakeries. Never
>  counted, tens of thousands of ashtrays.*

Photo #3: The Midtown Fires, 1944

During the invasion
of January, the year begins

with the flickering firefights
of uncertain outcome.

Trailer flames, hutment blazes—
Every neighborhood in Oak Ridge

lights up the epidemic year,
nearly a thousand alarms

despite the trained caution
of every resident.

An hour or more, each night,
some lie awake like watchmen

for the burglary of fire.
Children are slapped, sometimes,

for carelessness. Out of love.
Out of inevitability.

Someone's hands always shake
over kerosene, the fuel so

necessary, the inexperienced
are forced to defuse.

As if daily sacrifice was required
by the American version of God.

As if the trailers were set
on altars fashioned by faith,

the temporary triumph of flame
across a street or distant

as an accidental Passover,
the fortunate rising

to reignite before walking
to incomprehensible work

with discipline, resignation,
and yes, with joy.

> *Without preference, the chapel serves all*
> *the Protestant sects, Catholics, and Jews.*

### Photo #4: Square Through in Oak Ridge

Each Saturday night, in Oak Ridge, Bill Pierce
Calls squares for workers out for a good time
At the Midtown Rec Hall.  Comfortable
Or clumsy, the couples keep following
His lead. How quickly the city women

Have learned from rural friends, but their men are
As reluctant as boys at a school dance.
Do-si-do, Bill calls, now four ladies chain.
Behind him the fiddler has time to slip
In a pinch of chew tobacco. Later,
He has a sad solo when the dance turns
Slow and private, but now it's the simple
Refrains, the sound of shuffling and laughter
As Pierce works old-timey into his calls:
*Hey, all join hands and circle to the south,
And get a little moonshine in your mouth.*

This night, Pierce switches to wartime patter:
*Now allemande left with a soldier's wife.
If we finish our work, we'll save his life.*
The fiddler tells Pierce he misread a gauge
Into red. Thankfully, correctible,
The danger brief and only to himself.
*Luck is singing with a fiddle and bow.
All move together now, and do-si-do.*
Right now, there's time enough to celebrate
The unraveling of whatever's feared,
A near-rhyme for urgency's solitaire
With a single, mysterious lab task.
Pierce calls three familiar couplets to close,
And the fiddler holds the last note, then bows,
The necessity of the smallest share;
Any larger, impossible to bear.

> *In all of the dorms of the Secret City,
> the ironing rooms were for women only.*

Photo #5: Hutments Come to Oak Ridge

In Oak Ridge, races are separated
At the gate by the planned simplicity
Of expectations, the Negroes packed off
To hutments in Gamble Valley, their jobs
Requiring nothing more than dirty hands,
Heavy lifting, and huge humility.
Hutments, they learn, are sixteen by sixteen
Packing boxes. In each wall, one window
Without glass or screens, boards available
To shut out flies, mosquitoes, rain, and light.
What's more, Negro husbands are not allowed
To live with wives, and though they visit each
Other like prisoners, in the evenings
The wives are widows, the night as formless
As Genesis. So it's no surprise that
More than half the Negroes refuse those cells,
Choose to commute daily from Knoxville, but
Always, like migrants, driven in by bus,
Rebroken like badly set, fractured bones,
Searched each morning for weapons, contraband,
The remnants of reasons not to obey.
Always, through the translucent, stained windows,
They watch the guards gather as if woken
By alarms set so low in frequency,
They seem to insist from within like pulse.

*Gaseous diffusion plant K25 was, during the war, the world's largest building under one roof.*

## Photo #6: The Traveling Library in Oak Ridge, 1946

The children are eager for more pictures.
They scramble for warriors and princesses
Who will sometimes meet and love each other
Before or during or after battles.

Illustrated or not, none of the books
Mentions Oak Ridge, where those children's parents
Have begun to learn how they ended war
With obedience, discipline, and care.

Because science is a workday subject,
Because research never ends, these children
Will remain, three years yet, before the gates
Will open, all of them with time to learn

The new definition of infinite.
One of the boys is returning a book
Of horses, its gold-bordered cover torn
Through two pintos whose faces his mother

Has taped while he sobbed out apology.
Now, before the librarian reshelves
Those horses into circulation, she
Inspects for the interior damage

Of marginal notes, things scribbled as code.
Satisfied, she runs her finger along
The tape before pressing it to the boy's
Damp forehead as if she were knighting him.

*Cattle exposed to fallout from the A-Bomb test*
*in Socorro were shipped to Oak Ridge for study.*

Photo #7: The New Mexico Cattle, 1946

What's striking, at first, is that every cow
inside this rough-hewn corral is facing
the camera, curious as just-found
political prisoners. Slatted fencing
reveals an open landscape unlike where
those cattle absorbed the consequences
of the first atomic bomb. Scientists
are listening to *Inevitable's*
preliminary report. Everything
they observe and record is essential,
vital work, heavy with imperatives.
Not one of them has ever touched a cow,
but now they will keep them, especially
the yearling in the foreground who confirms
there is no limit to our emptiness.

> *After the war, Oak Ridge watched its story*
> *At the Grove—"The Beginning or the End?"*

Photo #8: The Girl Scouts Visit Oak Ridge, 1951

In full uniform, neckerchiefs and hats,
The Girl Scouts enter what's billed as sacred,
But the roads are unpaved, and though it's June,
They're muddy from recent rain, the ruts filled
With standing water, the ridges gooey.

The story ends, they all know, the summer
Before they started school, the final year
August didn't swirl toward apprehension.
Their leader, this morning, has related
How, during her junior year, the high school
Closed over Christmas vacation, saying,
"Just like that. No warning. Disappeared. Gone."

Look, right now they are afraid for their shoes,
Or worse, the misery of sudden slip.
The tour is just beginning, and Miss Spatz
Would never excuse anyone, not when
They have traveled thirteen miles, not after
The careful arrangements for permission
To examine, first hand, where the world changed.

Half of the girls love Frank Sinatra; half
Have been raised on Hank Williams. Four of them
Have televisions with snow-plagued channels
In their houses, and one has a father
Who tracks the frequency of A-bomb tests
In Nevada, the site remote as Mars.

Russians, he's said, know the end-time secrets.
For Christmas, her mother gave her dancing
Lessons; for her birthday, she renewed them
Like a subscription. When water covers
Her ankle, she leaps and squeals like science.

## Stunned

Sometimes, I've learned, the eyes of birds
Weigh more than their brains. Sometimes
Their bones weigh less than their feathers.

Sometimes, while touching her face,
I became a boy who believed
Her eyes exclaimed "Yes, go on,"

Because, undressed, she felt so light
Her luminous body lifted
Toward me, extraordinary

As the moment she became
An etched inscription on a plaque—
She was, she loved, she would have—

An odd conjugation of loss,
A wound in the air placed within
The private museum of the past

Just beyond the corridor
For longing where light is absorbed,
Where flight is interrupted

By the undeniable
Levitation of accident.

# Worship

*After a student's accidental death,*
*Her teacher, by hand, copies her poem*
*About the possibilities of love,*
*Reforming the imagery for desire*
*With intricate loops and decisive lines.*

    In Covington, Kentucky, on the grounds
    Of a Benedictine monastery,
    The monks built Monte Casino, forming,
    From limestone, the world's tiniest chapel.

*Her setting is the garden of St. Paul*
*Tended by two ancient nuns who, each day,*
*Inspect the light altered by arrangements*
*Of decorative trees, who prune, monthly,*
*The rose bushes to allow kneeling for*
*The raised right hand of a smiling Mary.*

    Six feet by nine, cell-sized, our group is told.
    Maximum occupancy three, a pew
    For each of us as if the secret phrase
    Is "save yourself," mote-swirled haze seeping through.

*Her lines are a gospel of surfaces,*
*Touch by touch where nerves nearly breach the skin.*
*They detail the sacrificial blossoms,*
*The needy topiary that shadows*
*The deep erosions from September's storms.*

    The single leaded window, the belfry
    Above too small for bells, and though we know
    A smaller church has recently been built
    On a deck in the center of a pond,

*And then, at last, shifting to a statue*
*Of the garden saint, his blessed hand smooth*
*From centuries of kisses, her poem*
*Ending in an astonishment of prayer*

    We study the history of this church,
    The monks moving on, replaced by vandals,
    And yet salvaged, brought here and restored, now
    Lovingly tended for our tiny joy.

# The Lengthening Radius for Hate

*Kent, Ohio*

I sat, one morning, on the grass
Where years before I'd survived
The guardsmen's volley. I sprawled
Beside a parking lot so long
I wondered why nobody
Questioned me. I could see the small,
Stone memorial to four dead
Students, the pagoda unchanged
On the hill's horizon. What was
I expecting while I became
My grandfather walking the mile
Of his lost mill where strikebreakers
Succeeded once, then failed? Or,
My father crossing the landfilled
Lot of his long-closed bakery
And recalling the gunman who thought
Robbing him would change his life.
Something stood here and then was gone—
Furnaces, ovens, armed men in gas masks,
The work we did from steel to bread
To books. I told myself I'd sit
Until somebody asked me why,
And morning slid past noon, women
And men moving to cars, pulling
Away, unwilling to answer.

*May 4: Luck, Skill*

Just often enough somebody comes back
From certain death, enough to make us think
We're the ones who will go on like my friend
Thrown clear of the T-Bird that exploded
On impact, the neighbor's boy who survived
Six minutes under cold water, even

Myself skidding into a four-wheel drift
Across a low median and both lanes
Of oncoming, rush-hour freeway traffic
Or sliding into the prone position
Across the asphalt of a parking lot
After a volley of gunfire began.
Going unscathed. Going upright again.
Nothing as miraculous as surviving
A free-fall ten thousand feet to a swamp.
I rejoined the loud, astonished traffic,
Not talking of escape like the pilot
Who'd landed a plane with a blown hatch door,
Ferrying a full manifest of ghosts
Back to the everyday task of living.

Safely on earth, the one in a thousand,
He spoke about trying to keep that plane
Alive, throttling up, working the small chance
Of improvisation while it banked left
And dove, drawn sideways and down by its wound.
"If I land this thing," he said to laughter,
Was the first phrase of a hurried promise
That ended with "all the rest of my life."
And then he started the full-time labor
Of silence about how, after those first
Minutes of surviving, he knew he would
Never again be so skillful, that it
Saddened him until he seemed an athlete
Just retired, his gratitude so awkward
And false he knew this was the first day of
The long sentence of dissatisfaction.

*Mother's Day, 1970*

"They should have shot you, too," my uncle said,
After I chose between the protesters
And the blunt authority of the Guard.
Sick of my mutton chops and thick mustache,
He hated how I thought I knew the world
Better than he did without picking up
A gun or grenade or the requisite
Gumption to wear a uniform with pride.
That Sunday I was back home from Kent State
Where classes had been canceled on account
Of jerks and whiners like me. My father,
The one brother of four who hadn't aimed
And fired at Nazis, sat silently through
That long oral exam for loyalty,
My uncle repeating, "Look at yourself,"
Like a therapist for family,
Waiting while I drifted to France where men
Who had followed him were guessing their odds
Against the higher ground of the Fascists,
Each of those men staring at my uncle
For the terrible, opened lips of "Go."

*All Through May 1970*

I hitchhiked, believing in the kingdom
Of rootlessness. I was naming myself
By choices, whether I wanted to be
Wounded or dead or the distance runner
Of regret. I carried a small, silly
Suitcase for personal items, saying
Nothing to bored or curious drivers
About my history of presidents
By name: Kennedy, the office-buyer;
Johnson, the quitter; Nixon, the liar,

Who had called my classmates "bums"
and killed them two hundred yards
from my Faulkner seminar at Kent.
I was waging the old revolution
Of flight, using the pity of strangers
And all of the name-calling that followed
Whiskey chased by beer. By the beginning
Of June, I rode home to re-up at Heinz,
Earning enough to start my last term of
Listening to the lectures of others.

*Where the Back Seat had been Removed*

In Ohio, near Youngstown, two short rides
Into hitching, I climbed inside a stranger's
Idling car, one ride closer to Pittsburgh,
And this driver promised me as far as
Sharon after he dropped off his cargo.
I might have panicked then, imagining
His claim an excuse for forced seclusion,
But he said, "What do you think's in there?"
Meaning the four steel cans he carried
Where the Ford's back seat had been removed.
Milk, I thought, but didn't guess, satisfied
With "No idea" before he said,
"Nitro" as if I'd believe anything.
"It don't abide shaking," he added,
And I told myself *not possible*
As he described how we would vanish
Like the Japs at Hiroshima, neither
Cruel nor clowning, just, as drivers did,
Making conversation to pass some miles.
There were railroad tracks we crossed so slowly
I had time to expect an imminent,

Personal hell, and yet I sat inside
That car while two strangers unloaded,
Repeating this couldn't be the day
For disaster, not when the work looked
As routine as the milkweed and burdock
That bordered the factory's loading dock,
The bare bulb of the sun suspended above
A lot so sparse with cars I believed
Most workers parked elsewhere so something
Of themselves would survive a mistake,
The small promise of the road straight south
To home from Sharon, Pennsylvania
As trivial as the curses those can loaders
Shouted so much in unison they seemed
To be chanting the stunted chorus
Of a well-known song while I listened
To my muscle and bone and voices
Saying the same things over and over
About the necessity of balance.

*Fraternity Brothers*

Two years, Rich Cook had lived across the hall,
Giving me rides in his damaged car
Where we breathed the stink left behind
By a creek that flash-flooded hood high,
But this summer Cook was a soldier
In the Ohio Guard, and I was
Reading the Victorians and Modern Dramas
At Kent State where classes had resumed.
Since my second beer, I'd been posturing
As a near-miss survivor, and now
Cook was drunk and angry and ready,
He said, to shoot me if history

Repeated itself. He had a pistol
In that flooded Ford I could see through
The screen door where white moths were frantic
To enter, and he wondered out loud
If I'd piss myself if he decided
To show-and-tell me just how cowardly
I could be up close with him and brother
Bowers just back from two tours and a pair
Of Purple Hearts, somebody who'd survived
Hamburger Hill and nameless night patrols.
Cook asked if I was a Communist now
Or just some big-mouth asshole drinking
His beer with someone who was worth a shit,
And I was ready to renounce my years
Of secondhand graduate essays,
All of those sweet-sounding platitudes
Seeming as simple as pre-meal prayers
While I was composing apologies
And expecting both brothers to lay
A combat-ready beating upon me.
I could say the overhead kitchen light
Beamed a Saint Paul moment of self-knowledge
And conversion, but what it did was
Flicker once when the refrigerator
Hummed into life just before Bowers
Said "Fuck the Guard" so matter-of-factly
I heard the period drop into place,
Ambushing one argument, at least,
In Youngstown where May was fishtailing
Into June, the three of us positioned
As if we were in our late-Sixties rooms,
A telephone hanging outside Cook's door,
The black receiver Cook had twice torn loose
And carried into my room after

Two a.m., both times silhouetted
Against the light, spitting, "It's for you."

*The Summer After*

I wore the company's washed boots.
I jammed my hair inside my hat
And pinned it like the old women
Who were first to arrive at church.

I walked fourteen cooling kettles
And carried long-stemmed spatulas
To scrape a shift's mixed cubes of meat
And vegetables, shake loose the salt.

I worked spaghetti with hot dogs,
Friday, four-thirty, the day shift
Backed up at three lights I could see
From the seventh story for soup.

That summer, there were new bosses
Back from the war that wanted me
As soon as I filled my transcript.
They sent me into boxcars where

The split bags of dried beans and flour
Roiled white dust around my face.
My second week, I had to kneel
In ice-watered blood to unclog

A set of drains.  For half a shift,
Pairs of men had hoisted frozen
Beef slabs, one hundred pounds per lift,
And they were long sick of wading
Ankle-deep. A fresh veteran
Repeated, "Clear the fucking things,"

Said, "Use your fingers" for the flesh
Half fat that thawed into the shape

And size of a hundred drain holes.
I felt for meat and pulled it free.
My other choice was unscrewing
The drain-lid, thrusting my arms to

The bottleneck built as backup.
On the loading docks, those men smoked
Facing the street. A set of tracks

Split the asphalt. The yellow-bricked
Warehouse rose so close, the sun's shift,
In June, was only ten till two.

*Late August*

At intermission, when smiling families
Flickered into the trees from the edges
Of the huge screen at Ranalli's Drive-In,
I rinsed my mouth with cheap wine and hooted
At the teenagers who sipped soft drinks while
Their happy-face snack foods skipped to the stars.
I needed to piss and pay for something
Salty for my new wife, who'd seemed bored
By Steve McQueen. In the men's room,
The cinderblocks repeated "Suck my dick."
The six light bulbs were yellow, one of them
Overhead when I leaned down to vomit
In the sink, my face jammed beneath the faucet
Until some high school boy in tie-dyed shorts
Looked so long I ripped my knees, right, then left,
Into the middle of his multi-colored crotch.
The boy said "Unhhh" and sat. I carried

Popcorn past a Plymouth where James Brown
Was groaning "Hot Pants" as if hips were toys.
Our speaker was face down in the gravel.
On the screen four hamburgers were dancing
Between two cheerful cups of Coke. I pulled
The damp cord, and the tinny trumpets that
Moved their tiny feet heaved up between us.

*The Casual Slurs*

Early in an evening of remembering death,
I tell my friend that after the Kent State shooting,
After students like me went home and waited out
Our anger, the police came armed to Jackson State
Like a recreation of the Ohio Guard.
They herded those students, I tell him. They backed them
Against the front wall of a dorm and suffered stones
And bricks until they opened fire as if they'd loved
The headlines from the week before, emulating
The Midwest's faux-army, sustaining their gunfire
Thirty seconds with an armory of weapons.

Almost five hundred times, I say, they hit that dorm.
Two dead, twelve wounded, all of them "nigger students"
According to the cop who called in the shooting.
That speaker's nickname was "goon," something history
Can't make up, his casual slurs, on tape, leaching
Into the voiceless future to poison language,
The violent separations that mark our speech
Though we've forgotten their indecipherable
Beginnings, ones like birth and the early years, what
We hear about from the mouths of those who love us,
Their stories working to share the unknowable.

*History Bites*

One night, in his room, complaining, my son
Sat to steal his report from the World Book,
List the Kent State dates and dead like fractions
To be reduced. "History Bites," it said
On his paper, "choose one, taste, and swallow,"
And I surprised him with slides, his father
The student who'd sampled his fresh mouthful
Of wartime after class. Monday, May 4,
Returned on his wall, and he worked the crowd
For someone familiar from the Dark Age
Of flared pants, long hair, and armies. Though I
Was faculty by now, standing in front
Of students with the rifle of language,
I wanted to show myself on his wall
Like some shadow animal of the hands—
Rabbit of the fingers, the knuckled dog,
Decorative pain of the headstone past.
Look, there I am then, I said, history
Whirring in that projector's fan. My son
Said, "What were you doing?" and I managed
"Watching," followed silence with "I don't know"
As if he were asking why I'd never
Left college or written one word on
History as it happened: Some roar of oaths
Striking the raised oath of rifles; some pop
Of gestures freeing the pop of gunfire—
Like fireworks, one platitude for anger,
And what I told my son was "Write this down":
We thought they were blanks; we stood ignorant
As some lost tribe staring at sticks that smoked.
Which is the way these histories happen,
Somebody saying "Never," "Of course not,"
Or its thousand variants. The crowd scene
That follows, the jostling forward of faith.

*Sequel*

The planets of difference seem
Perfectly centered, all of them
Preparing for an invasion.
Now each country walks in the paths
Of righteousness.  When the planes fly
Into our cities, my children
And theirs will call for the comfort
That comes from love.  We will listen
To each other's voices until
The world we have made together
Splits and scatters like providence.

## The Chernobyl Swallows

In April, near the anniversary
Of catastrophe, barn swallows returned,
Flying inside the exclusion zone to
Nest in the radioactive ruins.

Like disciples, the swaddled scientists
Marveled. The work crews, weeks later, toasted
The newly hatched, especially the fledged
With albino feathers after they soared

Like their siblings, devouring insects
With the ravenous hunger of swallows.
For months, the left-behind celebrated
How weak the worst was, and when the swallows,

No exceptions, flew southward, how feeble
Apocalypse could be. But come spring, not
One of the white-flecked birds returned, only
The ordinary nesting and spawning

Their own mutations. Families, by then,
Had moved back to where the world was quiet
And uncrowded, reclaiming rooms inside
The official radius of poison.

And through succeeding springs, no flight with white
Above them, just guards and squatters were left
To praise what they took for heroism,
Even if only among the swallows.

# Anniversary

If half of happiness is genetics,
What consolation there is in knowing
That some bees, now, prefer sex with orchids
That have evolved to irresistible.
Because bitterness ascends each evening
Like the moon. Because the leaves of house plants
Are dusted with fear as we tend to them.
Because we believed, once, that they adored
Our songs, that they and our unborn children
Were happier hearing those melodies.
Now my student, nineteen, says she's been raped;
Yours, eleven, is pregnant, yet we live
In an envied place. Now, epidemics
Of hive death have struck, local beekeepers
Repeating pollution and pesticides,
Proliferation of cell phone towers.
A white whale, nonfiction, has been sighted;
White rain has fallen on New Mexico.
In the museum we visited today,
A history of our sick presidents,
Their doctors and their treatments—pneumonia,
Ileitis, cancer, stroke. And what's more—
Bright's and Addison's Disease, depressions,
Their recoveries, deaths, and even so,
We were in Philadelphia, minutes
From the Liberty Bell and the tourists
Who travel here because we've muddled through
The way our early presidents came back
From bleeding a pint or more for fevers.
At last, when we looked at a killer's skull,
When we examined his brain in fluid,
I told you about the Nazi doctors
Who searched the brains of four hundred children
They had murdered to discover their dreams,

And you said "impossible" like a child.
Listen, butterflies and moths remember
Their lives as caterpillars, the hunger
And the constant dream of flight. Honeybees
Can recognize a face. Margaret Bell
Owned bees that flew five miles to mourn her death,
Gathering near her house for an hour.
If, as scientists tell us, most women
Are happier than men until they turn
Sadder at forty-eight, then here, writing now
Past sixty, I must believe my darkness
Is nothing like the midnight you suffer.
Someone, now, has made the blackest substance
Ever known, worse than the blind-dark of caves.
The world's dirt is disappearing faster
Than ever before. "Gary, just you wait,"
My mother promised me ten thousand times,
And I did until this moment, saying
That I've woken, love, to some happiness
All forty years in this bed beside you.

*The Mussolini Diaries* (2020)

# Fimbulwinter

When the polar bears come inland,
the sea ice thinned to insufficient
for their thick, white weight, we close
our schools and lock our children in
to keep them, for now, from harm.
Outside, the bears wander, dozens
as confused as our sons and daughters.
Winter, it seems, no longer lives here,
but no one has taught us where to go.

The sea, undressed, is not ashamed.
Our children churn their chilly rooms,
stir our houses until each one softens.
Each morning we wait for winter
to recover. The bears' breath clouds
our streets. Their pacing splashes mud
across their heavy thighs. Nothing lives
north of our village; we must not tell
our children that all of us are seals.

When rain continues, we marvel
how prophecy has deceived us.
This end is being preceded by
a succession of modest winters—
last year's, the year before, now this.
Yes, summer will vanish, but into
this constant, twilit season conceived
by gods we have never understood
until, surely, the long-promised wars
that bear them witness will begin.

## After the Election, Traditional Forms

My students are writing prayers, following
The forms of the ancients who expected
To be heard by more than eavesdroppers or
Family. Now they are considering
Their souls instead of marking their absence.
Doubt has drifted away from the table.
Mockery has left the room. Their ghazals
Contain refrains with Lord; their villanelles
Repeat: Resurrection brings white roses.
One writes a sequence of humility
In the metered lines of acquiescence.
Two finish devotion sonnets, saddened
By elections, afraid of those who hate
Aloud. On campus, they chant rhymed couplets
Of promises and march to the cadence
Of refugees. They hold their weeping signs
As if they were infants, wailing, at last,
The familiar litanies of longing,
The hallelujahs for their martyred hopes.

# Symmetry

A boy wearing a tie he has knotted
Perfectly on the seventh try listens
To his grandfather explain how there are
Caterpillars who consume exactly
One leaf before they spin themselves to change.

Don't worry, the grandfather says, the leaf
Is large, but the caterpillar must feed
Carefully to keep the shrinking surface
So symmetrical it seems undamaged
When seen from the sky by birds who target
Food by the irregularity of leaves.

Even for the simplest minds, it's never
Enough to be camouflaged by color.
Remember those careful worms outsmarting
Their predators. How, without proof, they sense
That their futures will have beauty and flight.

The boy? He twists his tie, stifles the sigh
Prompted by Sunday instruction, but now
Grandfather says, pay attention, there's more.
Plants are always listening, and they know
The differences among the vibrations
Caused by chewing, the wind, and the harmless

Disturbances of insects. Detecting
The work of caterpillars, they let loose
A surge of mustard oil that ruins
Their appetites, driving those predators
Elsewhere, leaving astonishment to us.

## Isolation

A day without news. Left behind,
last night's lead story—a friend's
untimely death, his son surviving
the head-on two miles from home.
This evening, my near-misses
an embarrassment of luck
inherited like wealth. Three times,
after our father died, my sister
sent half of his years-hidden stash
of bonds, CDs, or even cash
that was never enough for news.
My friend believed the news was
a woman so beautiful he would
never tire of her body.
It was like his love of drinking,
returning daily to that desire,
sometimes seeking my company
for an evening that extended
toward the blackout of any sort
of news. Maybe that need
is a form of loneliness
that catches in the throat
like a concealed confession
for the disquiet of restraint,
a moment when we are, at least,
in understanding's vicinity.
Outside, three steep miles of trail I
descend through forest. Apprehensive,
who wouldn't reminisce for comfort?
At 20:45, April 18, 1930,
the Wagner on the BBC,
as scheduled, was interrupted
for fifteen minutes of news.
Those listening to the radio

were worried, most likely, about
financial affairs, the way the world
was teetering toward another war,
but they heard "There is no news,"
and a piano began to play
as if nothing outside of their lives
had happened, and they could speak
to each other softly as the piano
continued, their living rooms
the extent of what mattered enough
to record and repeat, something
like the somber music after
Kennedy's assassination, each station
suddenly gone to cathedral organs,
bagpipes, and military bands,
all the instrumental ways
to indicate the news of loss
in the interlude between death
and its details through the static
of a distant station or the hum
that lives between frequencies.
In 1930, in radio's community,
every listener was intent upon
the first sign of interruption,
importance loitering outside,
even as the Wagner returned,
an aria at 21:00 without
the solace of excuses, one
by one shifting in their chairs
and beginning to whisper
as a woman cried beautifully
in song about unrequited desire.

## The Past Tense of the Census

In the census year, with three small children,
My wife sought part-time work, self-designed hours
Convincing her to canvas our county
Of farms and quiet, well-zoned streets. There were
Heads to count, assessment questions, and not
Every house, she soon learned, was welcoming.
House trailers were rare and always alone,
Set so often on barely landscaped lots
That she was surprised, this late afternoon,
By one site's borders of high wooden fence,
A lawn weed-infested, yet closely mown
By somebody, she thought, who was taking
Whatever care he could, not a man who
Opened his door and stood naked to show
Whatever news he might possess could wait.

Once exposed, a man might be capable
Of anything, logic that hurried her
To our car where she turned, keys posed to thrust,
And saw the trailer door closed, driving home
Touched only by a familiar story
During the year Jimmy Carter looked sad,
As if he understood another sort
Of census would defeat him—hostages
Held in Iran, inflation, scarcity
Of oil—though we spoke nothing of that
While our children scattered around our fenced-
In back yard, twilight settling, our neighbor's
Black Lab barking longingly at the gate
As my wife began, hushed and intimate,
To speak while we stood beside the deck rail
So our children could see we were watching.

What did he say? I asked. *He was soundless.*
What did he do? *He picked his teeth and spit.*
How close was he? *Arms' length. Able to reach.*
*I'm never counting him—is that a crime?*
And right there her story ended as if
She was willing to tear only one page
From her notebook of murmured memory.

Carter is smiling now, benign with age.
Though he must have more than such small horrors
To tell, the country exposed and ugly,
Taken hostage and held for limitless
Ransom. That man, years ago, was surely
Naked as he watched my wife, a stranger,
Cross his cropped-weed yard. And surely, he had
His chance to choose shorts and shirtless or call
Out "Just a moment" before fully clothed,
Choosing, instead, full-frontal exposure.
That evening, all we could see of our three
Children was movement. They appeared to be
Vanishing, about to no longer live
In our house, my wife using the past tense
Of the census to say, "He was, he was"
In a sentence stuttering, then gone dark.

# Sparklers

1

Once, at the museum's retrospective
for Kirlian photography, a display
of fingertips fringed by fire, captions
that claim light swells and shrinks
to expose our psychic auras.
Next, a torso surrounded by light
perhaps exuded by the holy spirit,
that body's corona proof we are
as chosen as the arrangements
of constellations, disregarding
that those suns cluster, we know,
by the accident of distance and size.

2

Decades ago, I wrote my name
on air with sparkler flares, circled
brief, eclipsed suns or threw
their violent lace into an arc
that spiraled sparks to our lawn
where, July 5$^{th}$, I had to find
every hurled wire from the night before.
Up and back, I paced our yard along
the narrow paths the mower took.
I failed, each year, to relight even
one wire, and some mornings, now,
I discover myself so thin and dark,
I fear I cannot be relit, even
by the acolyte of aging
in his white smock with scarlet hem.

3

One night, after baseball and the blasts
of complimentary fireworks
that opened nearly overhead,
the pedestrian bridge to Pittsburgh,

temporarily closed, compresses
our crowd of late-night walkers.
Someone next to my family
mentions the latest terror,
children and their mothers pierced
by an explosion of glittering spikes.
Faces of young girls illuminate
two nearby phones. Ahead of us
a father believes his arms
have invented safety.
The river's cruise ship passes
beneath us, its decks packed
with prom goers. The river reflects
a swirl of pinwheels; a vendor
ignites a fistful of sparklers.
Somewhere, terror dreams
our bodies as it decides
the exact address for delight.

4

Just now, I have learned that
some caves in New Zealand have
planetarium ceilings, their stars
systematized by the fixed, feeding
positions of glowworms, each
of those brilliant larvae claiming
a uniform space, spinning curtains
of threads to fish for food. Always,
in that ordered heaven, those worms
shine, their beacons drawing insects.
And sometimes, those larvae, transformed
at last, to clouds of gnats, are trapped
among the sticky filaments spun
by their children to be held and eaten.

# Contagious

*Dance Mania*

Within an early chapter
In the thick biography
Of hysteria, Frau Troffea
Suddenly lifts her arms
As if she's hanging laundry,
A spread-wide sheet. Hallelujah,
Perhaps, but then her feet
Skid into the swerve of dance,
Limbs chattering out of sync
With any tune her neighbors know.
There, in the sixteenth century,
Spectators gather like guests
For the first dance at weddings,
But she carries on for days, tranced
By some phantom partner
Who leads until someone joins,
Then another, so many more
In this weeks-long fit of dancing,
That ballroom fills four hundred strong,
Twisting to the inaudible,
The song on repeat, the pit keyed
To a frenzy of thrashing,
Each dancer with room enough
For solitary violence.
Nothing can end this except
Exhaustion or, for many, death,
The manic choreography
Famous for casualties
Who endured to the heart's collapse.

*Miss Howell Explains "Contagious"*

Twice a week, during public health,
Miss Howell filled the room with fear
While we sat in perfect rows marked
By small spots in the wax, the ones
That revealed restlessness, that shamed
If they showed like lace-edged slip hems.

The contagious, she said, leave filth
That lives on buses and streetcars
And seats at the Etna Theater.
What's worse, you'll never know who's been there
And given you the itch and fester.

The contagious, she said, shout words
You mustn't say. They seed their yards
With bottles, cans, and tires; drip snot
And never cover when they sneeze.
They wipe their noses on their sleeves
Where crusts collect like scabs that bleed.

The contagious borrow combs, touch fountains
With their mouths. They gobble food they've dropped
To floors. Not setting rings of paper,
They squat on public toilets, never scrub
With water that's been run to scalding hot.

The contagious are everywhere,
Common as flies. Splattering stains,
The contagious spread like lies.
Look around, you'll see what I mean.
Eyes open, class. Keep yourselves clean.

*Children's Television*

> *In Portugal, a children's soap opera produced mass hysteria, symptoms of the script's mysterious disease showing up in young viewers.*

Epidemic waits like the rocks
Below the cliff-carved narrow road.
It hums the synonyms
For inevitable, arranges them
In sentences slick with speed.

The script opens its sack of symptoms
To teach the country's children,
Each episode completed
Like homework. One mother fears
Permanent pockmarks; one follows
Her son's geometrical proof
Of cough and rash and fever,
Afraid of its solution.

All of them watch until the script
Declares an end to epidemic.
But after every child recovers,
After school reopens, parents
Learn that a child, next season,
Is crushed inside accident's car,
And all of them refuse to drive.

*The Devil's Children*

"The sins of your fathers," Miss Shaffer said,
"belong to you," and she listed the ways from drunk
to unfaithful while our Sunday school class
constructed heaven and hell, silently
attaching the future for all of us
onto the church's new bulletin boards.
Melanie Truman, whose father was gone,
cut narrow spaces into heaven's gate,
forming a grate so we could see inside
where white wings we drew floated against

a cloudless blue sky. We shaped a purple robe
for God and a loose, white cloak for Jesus,
their faces turned away because we dared
not look upon them. "The whirling of those white wings,"
Miss Shaffer said, "looks like it was created
by the sweet, benevolent breath of God."
All of us designed the black wings for hell.
Dick Wertz, his father arrested, scissored scarlet
triangles for eternal flames and left the green door
to hell wide open for the paired hands we made
by tracing ours. We forecast weather for hell,
heavy rain, every drop vanishing above the flames
because not one would ever reach us when
God saw into our sinful hearts that year
before boys and girls were separated
for Sunday School, before we began to learn
the sheer sins of lust and envy, using the sin
of falsehood to deny how we abused ourselves
and blasphemed, counting the commandments
we broke each day although Miss Shaffer made us sit,
one by one, beside the dark, detailed face
of Satan she drew, learning, each Sunday,
how it felt to be the devil's children.

*The Bug-bite Commonality*

> *In 1962, dressmakers in a textile factory blamed the bite*
> *of an unseen bug for the illness that spread among them.*

The dressmakers grew faint,
Unionized by the venom
Of a bug so elusive
The foreman had to search
Like a safety inspector.

Claims fluttered their small,
White wings until, at last,
Owners started the strip search
For evidence, bodies bared
For a physician's house call.

What, among insects, left
No mark as it poisoned?
Ask us, the dressmakers said.
Go ahead, and they answered
As if they'd taken vows

During suicide videos,
Each of them displaying
Scissors and needles,
Wearing a white mask
Over the nose and mouth.

When one of us dies, examine
Your flawless flesh. After the next,
Open her sewing machine
Like a music box, and its song
Will emerge like a spider.

*My Mother Lists the Things that are Catching*

Measles. Mumps. Chicken pox.
The flu. The common cold. Strep throat.
Whooping cough. Smallpox. Tuberculosis.
Head lice. Ringworm. Impetigo.
Poison ivy. Poison sumac. Poison oak.
Comic books. Television. Rock and roll.
Lying.  Stealing. Cursing. Idle hands.

*The Crusades*

One Sunday, just before we were moved to the next "higher" class, Mrs. Shaffer said the Crusades were the pinnacle of holiness. "Imagine," she said, "a host of armies fighting for Christ." She told us about Peter the Hermit, the hero who preached so well Christians everywhere joined up to rescue the Holy Land from the heathens. "Because the struggle never ends," she said, "so many Christians wanted to march to Jerusalem, there was always a next Crusade. In 1213, there were 30,000 children who marched. Imagine that, boys and girls. Imagine them being willing to be martyrs for Christ."

*The Trespasser Chronic*

Because my sister had walked home
alone eight Fridays that summer,
this time carrying the green skirt
she'd sewn at 4-H, mastering
a straight, invisible seam,
she took a short cut through the yards
of tiny, flood plain houses
bunched like a small, silent herd.
She was eager, in August,
to enter that skirt and a dress
in the county fair, girls' novice class,
hundreds of preteen outfits
laid out for three shades of ribbons
two weeks after she identified
which loose dog, possibly rabid,
had bitten her as she crossed
that neighborhood of the unleashed,
so hesitant, when she'd narrowed
the choice to two, that both were loaded
into a van while the owners cursed,
the rest of that pack of dogs
barking as if they were
marking her, as if, next time,
they'd make sure she'd never tell.

*Tulipomania*

In the early seventeenth century, in the Netherlands, tulips from Turkey charmed everyone. They loved Holland's soil. New breeds were coveted. The price of bulbs went up. There were mornings when so many people woke to what seemed like paradise, the rich had to own the best of those bulbs. Speculators in bulbs made huge profits, and buyers, eager to be rich, bought bulbs on credit. At last, the price of a bulb rose to as much as the equivalent of two million dollars. When the bubble burst, the deepest believers were ruined.

*Ugsomeness*

On television, politicians
Lift from disaster's leaves like starlings,
Their thick-flocked chatter sending shudders
Through the room of held drinks and hors d'oeuvres.

Somebody suggests, "Fear and loathing,"
Producing applause as if a book
Will follow that allusive title.
*Ugsomeness*, I tell them, the tough,
Archaic word better suited
To measure the circumference of rage,
And not willing to explain, I walk
Out the door and stare at the still life

Of the neighbor's house, time slowing down
Like accident's traffic, this loathing
Setting flares before it lifts its paws.
After a while the inside voices

Begin to smear like an overstrike.
Loud talk infects the living room, turning
From politics to the poor and dark who,
Quite frankly, they're tired of hearing about,

Someone shouting "ugsome!" and receiving
A spontaneous round of laughter.
For now, alone, there's a sensation
Of stillness that I understand is

The hell side of immortality,
This loathing so lame in familiar
English, yet extending as far as
The infinite integers for pi.

*The Space-Junk Premonition*
One autumn, my son searched the sky
For the first sign of space junk tumbling
Precisely toward us, sleeping downstairs
And walking eyes-up, expectant.

He researched each satellite,
Its size and orbit. He prophesized
At school, at last infecting
Boys and girls with binoculars

Who, for hours, scanned overhead,
A pinpoint of hysteria
In Selinsgrove, Pennsylvania
Where they anticipated craters

As if they were following
Invasion bulletins. Each of them
Slept in their basements, and each woke
Believing a terror of fragments

Had torn apart someone they loved,
A skeptic in an upstairs room.

*A Citizenry of Birds*

My neighbor, shortly after sunrise,
Says he loves to hear English
In the morning from his backyard birds.

They're citizens, he tells me, born here,
So many generations
With us, their accents have disappeared.

His mouth flexes. The pink horizon
Has nearly vanished. We are
Surrounded by the bright eggs of May.

My nod, meant to be neutral, narrows
The distance to empathy.
Only our lawns show the paths of shoes.

Suddenly, along our street, houses
Are raising flags, becoming
The embassies of allied countries.

When a siren opens full-throated
On the nearby county road,
I try to translate its accident.

Squalled from his architecture of leaves,
Vowels seem a needle's cry
Seeking a sample of suspect blood.

Some of the letters cannot be sung;
His lawn displays the sparkling,
Bent admission to his blue-rimmed door.

*A Month of Crusaders*

| | |
|---|---|
| March 29th | Moscow, two women detonate on the Metro, 40 dead |
| March 31st | Kislyar, two bombers, 12 dead |
| March 31st | Khyber, Pakistan, one car bomber, 6 dead |
| April 4th | Baghdad, three car bombers, 42 dead |
| April 9th | Ingushetia, Russia, one woman detonates, 2 dead |
| April 12th | Mosul, Iraq, one car bomber, 3 dead |
| April 19th | Peshawar, Pakistan, one bomber, 26 dead |
| April 23rd | Baghdad one car bomber, 11 dead |
| April 26th | Sana'a, Yemen, one bomber, 1 dead |
| April 28th | Baghdad, two car bombers, 5 dead |

*Possession*

In the 17th century, in Loudun, Mother Superior Jeanne des Agnes claimed the spirit of Urbain Grandier, the parish priest, visited her at night to seduce her. Soon other nuns reported spectral foreplay, moaning in ecstasy at night, convulsing and speaking in tongues during the day. Exorcism followed, but the nuns remained possessed by the demons Asmodeus and Zabulon who had entered the convent with a bouquet of roses thrown over the wall by Grandier. When possession went public, crowds of thousands come to watch. Out of the nuns' mouths flowed public blasphemy. From the files of the exorcist came the contract from Asmodeus himself, signed in blood by Grandier, a host of demons, and Satan himself. That contract has been saved for centuries, so that long after Grandier was burned at the stake, those nuns recanting and regaining their holiness, we can witness Satan's pitchforked signature and the decorative names of the demons.

*The Martyr in our Town*

The martyr in our town is scouting
The public places where we gather
In great numbers. He enters our malls
And notes the busiest stores; he scans

The food court's longest lines. Fridays,
He watches football at the high school;
Saturdays, a blockbuster film.
Sundays, there are churches to attend,
Sitting with families on wooden pews.

The martyr in our town studies
Prophecies and commandments. He reads
Only the holy translations. At last,
When winter justifies his knee-length coat,
He thickens his waist with dynamite,
Develops a nails and ball-bearings paunch.
He enters the one restaurant where
Every diner has three forks, two spoons,
And wine on ice, ticking as he gives
His reservation-name. He decides
That the tables nearby are perfect
With use, steps forward as the hostess
Offers a complimentary room
For his heavy coat. All this, he prays,
Will spread, go airborne, a pandemic
Contagion. She employs the word "sir"
Just as he triggers himself, ascending.
1

# Hole in the Head: A Love Poem

*Performed as far back as the Stone Age, trepanning is
the world's oldest surgery*

In *USA Today*, back of her head
To the camera, my daughter pushes
Toward the door of a New York subway.
Six weeks after the towers tumbled, turned
Away from the lens, she's the next victim,
Her and the rest of those passengers who
Are fighting their way from explosion's smoke.

She expected the terrorists themselves
To loom out of the tunnel at the end
Of the Manhattan Bridge. "I thought," she says,
"A piece of something might open a hole
In the back of my head. All I could do
Was keep myself from falling to the floor."

2

A true story, the one about a man
Who tries to bore a tunnel through his skull,
Taking a drill to himself, twice failing
The dare of trepanning to harmony.

More truth—how his girlfriend assisted, how
She broke through, putting a hole in his head
So he overheard his brain, what sounded
Like air bubbles running under his skull.

We marvel now and shake our own sealed heads.
The girl friend records her do-it-yourself,
And there, on film, after she cuts her hair,
Her pet pigeon flutters as she opens.

Such slow, and careful, and bloody labor.
She stretches toward the lens, pinpointing
The approach, she says, of tranquility.
Though surely, I'm thinking now, we should be

Attempting self-surgery on our hearts,
Opening ourselves to longing and love,
Drilling until we look down, recording
The insistent turbulence of desire.

3

*You need these things like a hole in the head,*
My mother said, meaning comic books
And movies, records, extravagance.

*You need these things like a hole in the head,*
My father said, meaning vitamins,
More sleep, a remedy for asthma.

*You need these things like a hole in the head,*
My sister said, meaning boys who were
Fractured and girls with reputations.

*You need these things like a hole in the head,*
My teachers said, meaning cheating and
Failure, slouching, talking out of turn.

*You need these things like a hole in the head,*
My pastor said, meaning lust and greed,
Envy and sloth, pleasure, faithlessness.

*You need these things like a hole in the head,*
I told myself, meaning church and school,
Obedience, mortality, tears.

4

Three years old, sitting on a stool for dinner, my daughter rocked herself back, then forward, then back while I managed one "stop" and one "no" before the stool toppled backwards and she was flung toward the raised stone fireplace. I lunged, too late, and saw she'd missed splitting the back of her head by less than an inch. Her skull intact, she stared up at me. For weeks, that spot a finger's width from the right angle of stone demanded my eyes down as I passed, offering terror and relief. Though years later, my student fell on a flight of stone stairs, her head snapping exactly to the edge of a step with enough force to kill her.

5

After my student died, head wounded too
Badly for repair. After her parents
Were summoned for memorial, I stood
Beside her mother in the President's
Huge house clutching a crystal flute of wine
Like a bad excuse while she let me add
Stories to sentences of sympathy.
"God bless you," I thought she murmured, the words
A tiny packet of ash, the gesture
Of grief passed like hand-written testaments
From a foreign culture, and I began
To recite my history of the dead.
I did praise and promise that ended with
Proposing her daughter's name on a prize,
The room sparkling with embellishment's light,
That girl's mother listening while looking
At me as if I were folding a flag
Like a soldier, each of us donors now,
Natal, endowing the unbearable.

6

Hundreds of ancient skulls have been discovered with circular, measured holes. What headache would drive their owners to sit for the drill? What needed to be freed? Who, surviving, would come back for more? The questions brush our hair until we touch the Braille of ourselves, feeling the breath of the ancient Peruvian man who died, every one of the seven holes in his skull showing signs of healing.

7

For weeks, my daughter refused the subway.
She walked until the aftershocks of fear
Subsided to hums of vibration. When she
Boarded again, she recognized no one
From terror's footnote. "When my head is turned,"
She said, "I feel a killer's point of view."

As if it coughs a spray of contagion,
Her anxiety plows through every crowd
Until there is no vocabulary
For security. Just below bone lies
Who she's become. Love swirls into my throat.
When I open my mouth, I moan silence,
Seeing her head like a photographer.

8

One morning, holding a drill to my skull,
I trembled. Even that brief fantasy
Of forthrightness snatched my vision naked.
I was unbalanced by held breath, shut up,
The one who required a hole in the head
To imagine happiness. Like writing
Enough lines about love that at least once
I might finish with the words heading out,
Like a space probe's miscellany, toward
The possibility of connection.

*For Now, We Have Been Spared* (2025)

## The Art of Moulage

For dermatology, for the betterment
Of medical science, Joseph Towne produced
Over five hundred models of skin disease,
Forming those faces from beeswax and resin,
Applying disease with spatulas and knives--
Lesions and rashes, pustules, and the chancres
Of unchecked syphilis, especially those
On faces disfigured by heredity,
Bad luck, or unwisely satiated lust,

An art, getting sickness just right, and there were
Others, like Jules Baretta, who created
Two thousand moulages, some of which followed
The changes in flesh from first symptom to death.
What's necessary to warn us? Tumors? Wounds?
Neither of those masters would share the secrets
Of his work, refusing to teach the darkness
Of gangrene, the inflammation where it spreads.

My father, near ninety, declared his creased face
Unrecognizable. My friend's mother, whose
Beautiful face was shredded through a windshield,
Lifted her right hand to the dense thicket of scars
When someone approached. . . . Look, an hour ago,
The harelips splitting the faces of children
Made me turn a page of a news magazine,
Sending me back to the soft community
Of the unscarred that turns away, revolted,
From the terrible commonplace of acne
And shingles; from warts, boils, melanoma—
And yet, with models, we are fascinated
By the possibilities of the body,
What we are capable of turning into,
Misery thriving until our skin becomes
A sieve for horror that rises through the pores.

## After War News

This evening, in rural Pennsylvania,
a crowd forms near the storage lockers
abandoned by the nameless, dead maybe,
in prison or dementia, missing the rent
for so long nobody sympathizes
when the auction begins, a few dozen bids
thinning the signals until the price stalls
at fifteen hundred dollars, a better gamble
than a few months of lottery tickets.

The moon, lately, was a celebrity, full
and a few miles closer than usual, enough
to bring three neighbors outside near midnight.
One of them suggested "Auld Lang Syne,"
but I was alone with remembering
the approach of planet Melancholia,
how, for one perfect night, it was sized
exactly like the moon, the sky brilliant
with the fascination of malevolence.

A perigree moon, science calls it, tides
heaving higher, but those three neighbors
soon talked about televised storage wars,
excited by the unknown. One repeated
the story of how eleven hundred dollars
earned a vintage Corvette, and because
he had never been inside my house, I thought
of him bidding if it were foreclosed, how much
he'd risk for what he imagined I treasured.

Each spring our village sends trucks to collect
the objects we see as trash—a typewriter,
a VCR, a lawnmower, two rusted grills—
each of those hieroglyphic possessions

spelling what we will not store. Soon, the moon
ordinary, a fleet of cars and trucks will invade
our street, the scrupulous or poor permitted
to thin our garbage, value in so many ruins
that nearly all of the useless vanishes.

Lately and often, invasion drives the news.
When aid is tentative and tiny and slow,
the defenseless make weapons from trash.
This semester, a colleague has died
during class, the first day, when his students,
all freshmen, knew him only by name or
stories shared by veterans. One witness
said she could see silence, like a cloud,
smothering his body. The others nodded.

My father, who surrounded himself
with silence, taught the imagery of stars.
On clear nights, when I visited, he turned
talkative in the back yard, picking out
even the lesser-known constellations—
bird of paradise, eagle, whale, the two
hunting dogs that I accepted as his way
to enter paragraphs that introduced
stories set, as he aged, further in the past.

Surely, whatever faith he had would have
welcomed the news, this evening, that
cave paintings discovered in Europe
depict, not animals, but constellations.
That, from prehistory, there have been
metaphorical portraits of the distant,
the ceiling of the world decorated
by gods so generous they displayed

an encyclopedia of their dreams,
every pin prick of light with a purpose
waiting to be discovered by those
who risked the sharp-toothed and clawed.

The future was as unformed as heaven,
a wish in need of language. Idea,
not yet named, was about to be born,
its shape evoked in unreliable light.
A chant, at last, rose from the others
in a smoke-choked cave, a syllable
repeated with the hum of approval.
Though such comfort proved elusive,
the land violent and cruel, so little
to be done about suffering despite
spears and clubs readied nearby,
whatever else might be said lost
in eviction or death, that gallery
given over, as it often is, to brutes.

# Upon the Death of Sons: An Elegy

*"No one believes that to die is beautiful . . . we console each other though we have been spared."*
—Philip Levine

*The Father's News*

He has lost a second son,
the first at twenty, yesterday
at forty, as if round numbers,
decades apart, had been cursed
by a long, cruel, deliberate con,
and we, acquaintances and friends,
join together in chorus,
our condolences changing
as little as prayer, our language,
interrogated by catastrophe's police,
unable to form an alibi for God.

1
*Underground*

In a museum dedicated
to man-made landscapes,
a virtual elevator
lowered his family through
the Earth's calibrated crust,
the temperature rising
from coal mine to gold mine
to the deepest bore hole,
each with a verified heat
until they were safely in hell.
They did not descend
to the death of sons;
nobody said a word
about anything but flame,
the childish horror that
is taught like spelling.

*Consolation*

Giraffes, until now, considered
mute, have had their voices
recorded in a Viennese zoo.
They hum to each other at night,
the frequency so low that no one
had suspected. For comfort,
the zookeeper has guessed,
although he admits uncertainty.

2
*Desert*

Once, visiting Joshua Tree
in August, he woke his sons,
early morning already at
one hundred and six degrees.
Outside, both boys stood stunned
by what living things can stand
from a constant sky, and though
the park was posted like a building
officially condemned, others, too,
were willing to enter, a clutch
of hushed tourists wandering
among gravely threatened trees.
Even these adaptive trees
have limits, he told the boys.
What's more, they are vanishing
in an orderly way, the last
to die those that flourished
at elevation, torrid scaling that
natural defense like a Sherpa
leading extinction's assault team.

*Consolation*

His colleague says she has been
practicing "feeling" to prepare
for the trauma of failing students.
Throughout the spring, she has
rehearsed for her mother's passing.
To calculate the responses to
her own death, she remembers
herself in the third person.

3
*Park*

When the township ballpark had been
restored, the infield dragged and rolled,
he walked the treated lawn of center field
to where a slide and swings were set
in concrete beyond the wooden fence.
Both boys, unprompted, chose to scramble
along a jungle gym, ignoring April's view
of dried milkweed and goldenrod,
wild blackberries, sumac, a stand
of maples that shadowed a patch
of dark snow that he challenged them
to closely watch, staring and staring
to mark the moment it disappeared.

*Consolation*

Because blasphemy is like fair weather,
inevitable, without consequence.
Because we are taught never to do so.
Because there is pleasure in rebellion.
Because our bodies do not suffer, no
Blistering of the flesh or open wounds.
Because belief falters like the body.

Because we recognize its impotence.
Because the soul is a beautiful lie.
Because the gods are indifferent
to our children.  Because of
the merciless biology of the heart.
Because our words dissolve in air.

*4*
*Remnants*

A stroke victim in Portugal,
for years a widow, has lost
her sense of ownership,
jewelry and evening clothes
become roadside litter.
Now, not even her eight cats
seem hers, those surrogates
a mewling nuisance.
She is seventy-seven,
his father's age the winter
he opened a closet to show
him his dead brother's suits.
Like a clerk, he displayed
all seven one by one,
lifting each to the light
for extended appraisal.
"Your boys are his size,"
he said, expecting him
to welcome opportunity.
Near the door, laid across
an overstuffed, blue chair,
were two decorative canes
his father had accepted
after receiving the gift
of heart bypass wrapped
intricately inside a small,
but expensive box of time.

*Consolation*

Sometimes, a second language
is necessary for what's intended,
the longing for impossible just
beyond the borders of English.
*Tesknota*, 'the pain of distance"
in Polish, a longing, beyond
nostalgia, for more than the past.

5
*Birthdays*

The morning each boy turns ten,
It is raining, but expected to clear
By noon, sunny, humid, both beside
Water, premonitions in a distant country.
One boy is fascinated by knots, the other
Loves the strokes of the medley relay.
One bedroom wall displays bowline
And square, sheepshank, clove hitch,
And tripod lashing, all those twisted cords
Arranged under glass like monarchs.
Another celebrates the recent heroes
Of freestyle, butterfly, breast, and back.
Before those birthdays end, he rounds
Them up to clear and warm, twilight paired
With fireflies, full darkness with promises.

*Consolation*

Because we listen to nothing else
When our bodies clench and stiffen,
Our blood thickening in our throats,
We can only hurl and thrust, each
Object a weapon—Chairs, dishes,
Cue stick and fist—the legs unwilling,
Refusing to leave the breakage
And scars until we have raged
Long enough not to damage
Someone who is closer than ghosts.

6
*Science*

Two boys created a stew
of cafeteria food, bits of bread
and fruit, filling a paper cup
and sliding it into the hollow
of a spill-stained table leg.
Then they waited, eating
only brown-bagged lunches
above that school-bought brew.
This was science patience,
sandwiches and desserts
before they raised that table
on the seventh day, nudging
that tiny womb into the light
expecting the fine hair of mold
their recipe grew with darkness,
time, and heat, astonished as
a flurry of fruit flies lifted from
that soggy cup as if they had
fathered them, a sudden cloud
that fluttered and disappeared.

*Consolation*

This is the week he discovers the pitch
Of the blue whale's songs is getting lower.
This is the week mosquitoes swarm,
Their numbers swollen by record rain,
And yet science has learned these pests
Choose mates who harmonize perfectly
With them, enhancing the couplings
That bring some small equivalent of joy.

7
*Rapture*

He has listened, lately, to someone
Explain mindfulness at a dedication,
The rooms named for a colleague
Who has died by suicide, a woman
Who, each term, asked her classes
To write their thoughts in columns:
*To be done. Maybe later. To delete.*
Now send the erasable into space,
She would say, creating the rapture
For distractions. Those rooms had been
Refurbished like an abandoned mall.
Her father narrated her last weeks,
The sporadic phone calls farther
And farther apart like hospice breaths
Until, he finished, there were no more.

*Consolation*

Our nerves, science says, produce
The greatest pleasure when stroked
Four to five centimeters per second,
Though just now, he does not say this,
Not mentioning distance and speed,
The mathematics of ecstasy,
The encouragement of desire.

*Now*

He dreams, each evening, only of family,
his wife a frequent character, the voice
of his daughter, childlike, from the doorway
after midnight, her questions progressing,
phrase by phrase, from anxiety to fear.
His wife approaches like a survivor
emerging from catastrophe, their street
always behind her, its devastation
obscured by swirling fog or smoke.
His sons appear in their former rooms,
searching for things they hid when young,
toy cars and tiny, coded, secret notes
wedged in where they would survive,
untouched, forever. Both boys sleep
as late as vampires. Always, they return
at night like livestock. Though each dream
ends in limbo, his wife still advances
with sorrow in her arms, his daughter
still calls, his sons are always silent
overheard, moving from room to room.

## My Daughter, Talking about Boys

My daughter, talking about boys who drove her,
Mentions the one who sported a demo
From his father's dealership, the license plate
Exposing him like a badly made fake ID.
Together, we laugh, amusement not shared
The year she turned fourteen, that boy a senior
Who idled in the driveway like she was stealing
Something worth waiting for from our house.

Three have been mentioned before: The one
Who loved her art, who painted beside her
And failed the leukemia blood test, dying
Before graduation. The one, insulin
Dependent, who drank himself into coma,
Recovered, and starred in several sequels.
The one who called from the distant city
Of late-night melancholy, singing songs
That featured regret and need, who still
Calls sporadically, his voice thin and dim
As if it's passed through an atmosphere
Of years like the residue of meteors.

This late afternoon we are watching
Her beautiful teenage daughters swim.
Their father, the last of those boys, still
Texts, always after midnight, messages
That begin "Let's meet" before they skid,
Each time, from sentimentality to rage.
Now she, past forty, swells with the child
Of her second husband who has seemed
So stable his story is told in silence,
Making room, while she speaks, for the boy
Who sped her to a Saturday movie as if
The theater was an emergency room,

Then called a classmate the following week
And drove her into a skid and rollover
Off a country road, head trauma enough
To kill her. This story, until now, she has
Never told me, bringing it up at poolside
A quarter century later, because that driver
Has been discovered dead, cause unknown,
In a country where English is seldom spoken
Or even carried through customs like
A valuable history to be declared.

## Choosing a Trail

A multiple-choice test is posted near
the trailhead entrance, answers descending
from most difficult to wheelchair access,
and you consider your knees and back,
just how demanding steep climbs could be,
whether what is called uncertain footing
could be near the edge of precipitous drops.
For experienced hikers, your selection says,
and because you do not believe in irony,
you are soon grasping available branches
or going nearly to your knees for balance,
grateful the trail is so sparsely traveled,
you can discreetly acquiesce to need.
Less than five minutes, it takes, to reach
the trail marker for regret, the path ahead
void of everything but stones and shadow
and the approach of returning hikers.
You steady yourself into what might pass
for politeness, one hand gripping a gnarl
of outcrop, the other half-raised as if
you recognize the oncoming couple
whose two boys look eleven or twelve,
tenderfeet scrambling past, their parents
smiling your way like nurses before
they vanish. Briefly now, you are alone,
an opportunity, unseen, to pivot
and retreat a few hundred feet of downslope,
exiting that trail like a marathon cheat who,
you tell yourself, has the decency to claim
nothing but completing the course,
not even acknowledging the inquiries
of just-arriving strangers who ask
about the rope bridge over the gorge
and the spectacular three-tiered waterfall.

Head down, you slip among the elderly
who crowd the wide, mulched trail
that passes, after gradual descent,
beneath that narrow, swaying bridge,
observable from above but so far below
none of the hikers you silently passed
can identify you now that you have
removed your distinctly colored hat.

# Unmoored

Last night, explosion in a neighbor's garage,
The fire consuming the bulk of their house
Before hoses were unspooled. This morning,
The damage visible from our upstairs windows.
Sometimes, we manage weeks without thinking
That what we are is temporary. Have you
Ever sheltered in place, ominous clouds
Tinted bruise-green, the wind carrying what
Has been forecasted as a ruin of heavy rain?
I'm talking about a place where the highway
In and out of danger floods so often that
River sediment seems its surface. Where,
Falling asleep during downpours is like
Leaving active flames in your fireplace
Like my father did, trusting the cheap grate.
There is a story my worst students loved.
A father and son travel by boat to an island
Exposed by low tide. The small skiff, secured
Improperly by the boy, drifts away. Nothing
Can save them, yet none of the students
Ever blamed the boy for his fatal error.
What they loved to talk about was how
The father lifted the boy to his shoulders
And steeled himself as the ocean water rose.
The students, seventeen and often sullen,
Waved their hands to volunteer stories
Of their own about making terrible mistakes.
In that town, years before, a family had made
A fortune manufacturing Jello. Even then,
Two of the dead eyes of its factory windows
Remained unbroken. None of the boys would
Admit to liking Jello, but among those students
Were many children and grandchildren
Of men and women who had once believed

In the longevity of their work with sugar,
Powder, and dye. Even then, years before
The factory became unmoored, they would
Tell themselves that inevitability had not
Already begun. What they made so cheap
And colorful that it would always be boxed
For delivery within their neighborhood.

Now, a museum for what the town has lost
Is housed across from that high school,
As proximate as the fire-ruined house,
Its owners unmoored so catastrophically
That they chorus, "Who could ever imagine?"
As if stupefied, sounding like my father,
The widower, who, for decades, was stunned
To be living alone. Each time I visited,
He sank more deeply into the only chair
He ever used, his eyes sweeping the walls
Of the small living room as he murmured,
"Who would have thought?" Something I said
Aloud, just before sunrise this morning,
As I walked, uneasy, by my neighbors' yard
Into a dedicated, half hour of solitude.
Though, when I returned home, the low sun,
From a cloudless sky, cast the shadow
Of the undamaged, next-door house over
The scattered debris as accidental
As what remained of the impossible.

# On the Eve of the Presidential Election

Seven days before this store will open,
A woman has been caught on camera
Emptying another employee's purse,
Both of them trainees for bath-oil sales,
Soap and shampoo, beautiful, thick towels.
New jobs created, the window sign says,
The shelves stocked with grand-opening prices.
In the department store next door, there are
Two aisles for toiletries, purses resting
In eleven carts I pass, cameras
Along the walls. Eighteen televisions
Show the faces of this year's candidates,
Their last-day voices muted to puzzles.
To win our endless war, one candidate
Has said, we should target cultural sites,
Mentioning gods with exotic names and
Ancient, elaborate, crowded churches.
He has said shock, awe and Armageddon
As if he, himself, were a god reborn.

Earlier, a young aide displayed my town
On a screen centered upon her steel desk.
She zoomed to my street, enlarging my house
Until I was afraid my wife would walk
Outside to a looming war's consequence
Of cameras. Suddenly, my address
Looked so much a target I was nearly
Afraid to drive home. The candidate's name
Circled the red mug that woman sipped from.
When she said, "I can't stop looking," her voice
Seemed full of coded launch codes for weapons.

My father, one night, was robbed, at gunpoint,
Of sixty-seven dollars, the same year
I watched a boy my age steal six records.
He'd promised one of them for me, wanting
Nothing In return but my knowing that
What I loved to listen to had been free.
Our drones, the candidate says, can pinpoint
And attack the souls of foreign nations.
Any small idea can be nurtured
Until it matches an attractive name.
I know a woman, now, whose job it is
To pretend to be a customer while
Searching each aisle for shoplifters. Soon,
Each terrible thought will be photographed.
Tomorrow half of these shoppers will not vote.

# Advent

One early evening, in France, my wife
and I mistook the direction of a bus,
boarded, and rode until it emptied.
Idling in place, the driver waved us
forward to name our destination.
With gestures, he said that his shift
had ended, his bus scheduled to be
garaged nowhere near that address.
"You wait here," he said in English,
"quinze minutes," closing the doors.

By now, each of the last passengers
to disembark had disappeared. Nearby,
three dumpsters, a stripped skeleton
of a car poised as if collection was
expected. Isolated, the apartments
seemed to have been erected
as if a neighborhood would follow.
Their shadows groped for us, twilight
speeding from tangerine to purple.

Young men loitered where a bench
and shelter were a makeshift lounge.
The driver, we understood, had dropped
us at a stop sign, sparing juxtaposition.
From behind the apartments, a plane
struggled into the sky. Just before
quinze minutes had passed, every
shadow was devoured by sunset.

From the opposite way, a bus labored
uphill so slowly it promised breakdown.
Each seat was deserted. The driver
shook his head at our English.

What we did was lean forward from
the seat behind him, fixed upon
the wish to travel into our recent past
of restaurants, shops, and light.

What we settled for was the bus filling
with a flush of English, a possible end
to our deadlock with reasonable doubt,
a story so commonplace it could
fill every general admission seat,
no matter the size of the stadium.

For example, early this morning, along
our street, someone in a logoed van
emptied shopping bags of groceries
onto the front porches of our houses,
arranging them like laboratory samples.
From our angle, they glowed as if
insulated with light. We waited for hours
to touch them. We handled the produce
as if it were smeared with a sheen
of malignancy measured by its half-life,
made radioactive by foreign infection.

# Pentecostal

For unwelcome sounds, the single mother keeps a German Shepherd. Car door slams. Voices passing on the street below. The wind driving a deck chair against the sliding, glass door. Mostly, for the threats she does not hear. Preparation, like wine, is often paired with prudence. She reinforces the dog with a motion sensor. Coyotes, some nights, rouse the dog to barking before frightening the mother's floodlight to brilliance; her daughters, seven and nine, have grown into sleep that disregards her alarm.

This evening, the coyotes, as if they have memorized where light begins, pace at the edge of darkness while the dog, as always, does his extended solo. Even when they retreat, the dog is so dissatisfied, the mother leashes him and steps outside. Across the highway and from beyond the hillside houses that end in wilderness, the glow of wildfire has lengthened the radio's menu of languages. Fuego salvaje. Chay rung. Incendios. Smoke has drifted into the neighborhood. Evacuation is possible.

The empty lot next door has been cleared of brush and damage to lessen the chance of attracting embers. As if emptied, every nearby house is darkened, the ordinary and the reasonable already elsewhere or at rest. But carrying an axe, a neighbor has climbed her stairs to declare he will kill her dog and anyone who tries to stop him. The dog is a lunge of howls. The spotlight scorches them. The girls, holding hands, appear behind her but do not speak. The neighbor crouches, a gargoyle for the unbearable, four steps, then three, between him and the entrance to the radius of the axe handle he hefts slowly from left to right. For a moment, hysteria will not shut up. From somewhere close, a car alarm begins to moan inside a garage like a steady pulse. From house to house, barking erupts, testimony in run-on lines awaiting reason. Each flaring light translates those speeches, not into salvation, but, for now, reprieve.

## Walking Backwards

In the kitchen, sometimes, my wife
retreats, but mostly in the living room,
happy to have six additional steps
for walking backwards ten minutes,
meaning to postpone unsteady and
mustering a smile when she manages
back and back again with grace.

Agreed, the legs are vital, stories
of hip-breaking falls already stored
on retirement's flash-drive, friends
taking that giant step toward the line
where chance, so ironical, chooses
baby steps to decide each winner,
and yet I default to a skepticism
so shallow it surfaces as parody.

Agreed, she knows there are often
days when darkness refuses to lift,
and I use pedal and climb as relief,
and yet, I have never confessed how,
each time, I spin my digital pulse
into the age-calibrated red zone,
the range marked "conditioning"
ten years ago, before backing off,
thrilled and terrified and cleared.

But yes, there are evenings when
her walking is a thread that binds us,
both of us counting our steps together
without feeling behind ourselves
for the bookcase or the wall devoted
to art, doing this simple line dance
to the rhythm of apprehension's melody,
hearing time's chorus hummed into
our ears, the one so familiar
we automatically mouth the lyrics,
walking backwards to its music,
following the lead that waltzes us
in a tempo so comfortable we barely
sense the tiny increments of change
and balance seems enough for joy.

## Missing: A Psalm

Had the boy, such a smart five-year-old, not unlocked a door and walked away.
Had his mother not been bedridden by fever in their upstairs, rented rooms.
Had the boy, for half an hour, not bounced a rubber ball off a vacant building.
Had his aunt not arrived to nurse her sister and noticed, at once, his absence.
Had the boy, by this time, not been thirsty. Had his mother not begun to cry.

Had the boy not asked for a glass of ice water at a nearby store.
Had the man who sold ice cream not shouted, "Buy something or leave."
Had the boy's mother not said, "Where on earth could he have gone to?"
Had he not meandered to the A&P to drink from its ice-cold fountain.
Had his aunt not walked fruitlessly to each room's windows.

Had a creek and railroad tracks not been near the grocery.
Had the boy not followed them past the mill to the river.
Had his aunt, after an hour, not called the police.
Had she not been told to "give the boy longer to show up."
Had the boy, for fifteen minutes, not tossed stones into the reeking water.

Had the boy's mother not read him his father's letters from the war.
Had another boy, a year before, not drowned in that creek.
Had the boy not retraced his steps from railroad tie to railroad tie.
Had those letters not taught the boy loneliness.
Had another boy, a month before, not fallen under a train.

Had those letters from far away not stopped.
Had another boy, the week before, not been abducted and killed.
Had his mother not feared for the boy's life.
Had the boy not imagined being missing in action like his father.
Had his aunt not sat sentry for news.

Had a man not waved and asked the boy where he lived.
Had the boy, eager for praise, not perfectly repeated his address.
Had the man not walked beside him along the tracks.
Had the tracks not paralleled the creek and a flourish of undergrowth.
Had the creek not dipped into a narrow, shrouded valley.

Had his mother not listened, with diminishing hope, for a door to open.
Had a man not been fishing in the shadows.
Had she not imagined a future of bloodhounds.
Had the fisherman not decided those two were not father and son.
Had he not called and scrambled up the weed-choked bank.

Had the friendly man not run.
Had the fisherman not refused the small boy's lead.
Had the boy's aunt not kept sitting sentry at the top of the stairs.
Had an alley not led to the house with upstairs rented rooms.
Had there not been a bell that rang when the boy entered like a customer.

Had his aunt not cursed, mistaking the stranger for a man with second thoughts.
Had that man not said he was a father, too, of boys who were small.
Had the boy's mother not appeared, swaying beside his aunt.
Had she not caught her balance.
Had she not quietly beckoned.

Had she not embraced him.
Had she not offered a choice between pizza and hot dogs.
Had she not poured him a glass of ice cold water
Had she not kissed his cheeks.
Had she not promised ice cream in a showcase of flavors.

## The Unicorn Lair

*Once, it was feared that exceeding the speed of sound meant a man might outfly his voice and strangle on his screams.*

Not laughing, a woman tells me
that the elusive entrance to
a unicorn lair has been found
in North Korea. Only now,
because their secrets are well-kept,
have we learned that skeletons
are being restored, beautiful
as anything in paradise.

Often, there are deceits disguised
so well for our desires they are
designed like myths: A magician,
for television, once vanished
the Statue of Liberty by
turning a crowd of witnesses
so slowly that a country of
viewers surrendered to wonder.

Always, in the dictionary
for easy dismissal, the list
of synonyms grows long enough
to seem countless, a collection
that soothes our lovable longings.
Our taste for myth and quackery
quickens our desire to embrace
each promising, suggestive hope.

For instance, such trust is enough
to pause me inside my office
in this house, now refurbished, where
a priest once lived within a set
of rooms so small anyone would
perceive them as a suite of cells.
Always, he had terriers, two
at a time, and, at last, cancer

no amount of praying could cure.
By then, a mile to the east, ground
had been broken, foundation laid
for the reconstruction of faith.
The rectory, vacant a year,
went dank and mildewed, cubicles
of shadows. The discarded church
became a clinic, its large lot

a gallery of patients' cars,
the near rows for the handicapped
and pregnant, a space fire-lane wide
for vans that transport the helpless.
In this small office transfigured
by students, I put aside work
for the leisure of thankfulness,
keeping fear and doubt priest-secret.

Listen, speed and velocity,
though often used as synonyms,
are not the same. Speed is travel
through time; velocity includes
the shift in position. Divide
your changes by the years it has
taken you to make them to learn
time is motion with memory.

Someone, after research, has learned
that the most common noun is Time.
Someone else, today, has written
to the paper claiming to know
how God prioritizes prayers,
responding from innocence to
brutality symbolized by
children and Russia's neo-czar.

He estimates five billion prayers
are mouthed per day, Time, happily,
a concept different for God.
Or Einstein, who declared that time,
as we approach the speed of light,
will slow until, after decades,
we will arc back younger than
grandchildren as if we have gained

the limitless advantage of
a now-shaken God. Consider,
now, that rocket flight. In the months
before he died, my father, past
ninety, remembered only what
he had seen first-hand, loneliness
his last lesson by example
how we disappear into Time.

Gary Fincke's poetry collections have won prizes from Ohio State, Arkansas, Michigan State, Stephen F. Austin, and Jacar Press. Individual poems have received the Bess Hokin Prize from *Poetry*, been reprinted twice by *Harper's*, and been selected for a Pushcart Prize. His books in other genres have won the Flannery O'Connor Prize for Short Fiction, the Elixir Press Fiction Prize, and the 2017 Robert C. Jones Prize for Nonfiction. Since 1984, he has published forty books of poetry, short fiction, and nonfiction, including a novel-in-stories *How Blasphemy Sounds to God* and the memoir *Amp'd: A Father's Backstage Pass*, an account of immersing himself in his younger son's life as the lead guitarist of the platinum-selling rock band Breaking Benjamin. He is the Emeritus Charles Degenstein Professor of Creative Writing at Susquehanna University, where he founded and then directed, for more than twenty years, the Writers Institute and the nationally recognized undergraduate creative writing major.

www.ingramcontent.com/pod-product-compliance
Lightning Source LLC
Chambersburg PA
CBHW021848230426
43671CB00006B/310